gaudí
of Barcelona

gaudí
of Barcelona

Adapted from the Spanish text by **Lluís Permanyer**
Photographs **Melba Levick**

RIZZOLI
NEW YORK

Photographic Credits

Arxiu Dr. Comas Llaberia, pp. 11 and 14.
Arxiu Nacional de Catalunya. Fons Brangulí, p. 6.
Francesc Català-Roca, p. 17.
Museu Comarcal Salvador Vilaseca, Reus, p. 185.
Pere Vivas, pp. 15, 125 and 150 above.

*The publishers and authors would also like to express their gratitude
to the following individuals and institutions who have permitted
photographs to be taken of the buildings reproduced in this book:*
Casa Batlló
Càtedra Gaudí
Col·legi de Santa Teresa de Jesús
Diputació de Barcelona
Fundació Caixa de Catalunya
Lluís Guilera Soler
Fabiola Jover de Herrero
Junta Constructora del Temple de la Sagrada Família
Santiago Llensa Boyer
Parròquia del Sagrat Cor, Santa Coloma de Cervelló

First published in the United States of America in 1997 by

RIZZOLI INTERNATIONAL PUBLICATIONS, INC.

300 Park Avenue South, New York, NY 10010

First published in Spain in 1996 by

Ediciones Polígrafa, S. A.

Balmes 54, 08007 Barcelona

© 1996 Ediciones Polígrafa, S. A.
© Photographs: Melba Levick
© Original Spanish text: Lluís Permanyer
Designed by Estudi Carme Vives
English text adapted and edited by Sarah Underhill

I.S.B.N.: 8478–2062–9

Colour separations by Alfacrom, Barcelona
Printed in Spain by Filabo, S. A., Sant Joan Despí (Barcelona)
Dep. Leg.: B. 22.837–1997

Contents

Gaudí (right) at Barcelona Cathedral during the Corpus Christi procession, June 11, 1924.

The Man and the City

Gaudí was fortunate to have lived at a time in which he received the patronage of clients who gave him a great deal of latitude, financially and aesthetically, to produce audacious and often unorthodox work. He caught the attention of prominent members of a bourgeoisie that enjoyed ever-increasing prosperity, self-confident men who wanted to distinguish themselves in every way possible. These successful merchants and industrialists found in architecture not only a form of investment, but also a significant and visible medium through which to convey their identity.

Gaudí also had the freedom to explore a variety of building types, from residential to ecclesiastical, without the scope of his vision being restricted by site limitations. I cannot help imagining how different his work might have been in the densely populated Barcelona of a few decades earlier, crammed as it was inside the city walls. Projects such as Park Güell, the Sagrada Família church, and Casa Milà would never have been created. We might also wonder whether in the narrow streets of the walled city he would have conceived facades such as that of Casa Batlló, which was intended to be seen from a distance. At the time Gaudí was receiving commissions, Ildefons Cerdà was planning the city extension laid out on the grid system, which made more land available for development in Barcelona than in any other major European city at the time. Wealthy individuals and their architects had at their disposal areas previously outside the city's perimeter, and thus the astonishing spectacle of the area of Barcelona known as the Eixample took shape.

This was also the period when Catalonia had firmly embarked on the recovery of its political independence, of which it had been deprived in 1714 by Philip V when the Catalans sided with his chief rival, the Archduke Charles, in the War of Spanish Succession. Central to this movement, known as the *Renaixença*, was a search for a strong regional identity, and it brought about a cultural and economic resurgence.

There are those who believe that Gaudí was lucky to have been practising during the height of *Modernisme*, the artistic and architectural style that was the Catalan version of the Art Nouveau and Jugendstil movements; personally, I am not so sure. I do not believe that Gaudí could be labelled a *modernista* architect. He certainly benefitted from having lived in a period of such splendour and creative fervour, above all in the applied arts, as he was able to collaborate with extremely talented artists and craftsmen. Some of his work does express *modernista* characteristics, but his unorthodox and inventive design solutions defy such categorisation.

Antoni Gaudí i Cornet was born on June 25, 1852. While it is still not certain whether he came into this world in Reus or in Riudoms, a small village only four kilometres from the city, documentary evidence points to Reus. Natives of this region were said to be "*Gent del Camp, gent del llamp* (People from El Camp, people of lightning)." Strength, determination, obstinacy, and tenacity were among their traits, and these were certainly characteristics of Gaudí's personality. Throughout his architectural career he acted as a true *reusenc*, making no concessions regarding his aesthetic beliefs, despite conflicts that arose with clients, critics, and the press; in fact, much of society at the time did not understand or appreciate his artistic vision. He staunchly stood his ground in the face of incomprehension and opposition, and his architecture was eventually accepted. On one occasion he claimed that he had managed to overcome all of his defects save one: his irascibility.

I believe that, as his career evolved, he positively cultivated it.

Gaudí's father was a coppersmith, and the architect claimed he was thus endowed with a sense of space that gave him the ability to think directly in three dimensions, which was less restrictive than the two dimensions used when drawing up plans.

An event of capital importance took place in 1869: he was sent to a school in Barcelona to complete his secondary education. From that moment onwards, Gaudí made his home in the city that provided him with the opportunity to make contacts, gain access to valuable sources of information, and meet artisans with whom he would collaborate and businessmen who would become his clients and patrons. Here, too, he had at his disposal sites on which he could transform his dreams into buildings that would occupy their rightful place in the history of world architecture.

Both at secondary school and at the Escola d'Arquitectura, Gaudí excelled in some disciplines while declaring himself uninterested in or incapable of understanding others, to the extent that one of his professors declared that he did not know whether he was in the presence of a genius or a lunatic. Gaudí had serious problems with spelling and proved to be only a mediocre draughtsman. Moreover, he was a pupil who did not recognise his teachers as masters and dared to contradict them. This gives us an early glimpse of the architect who would become known for his cutting rejoinders to powerful and influential people.

After completing his studies, Gaudí worked as a draughtsman for Francesc de Paula del Villar,

from whom he acquired no great knowledge, and who, ironically, he replaced as the architect of Sagrada Família. He also collaborated with Josep Fontserè, a professional he esteemed and respected, in whose studio he contributed to the realisation of certain details of the Ciutadella Park. Perhaps the architect who had the most influence on him was Joan Martorell, with whom Gaudí worked on a number of important Barcelona projects, such as the Jesuit church in Carrer de Casp and the Salesian convent in Passeig de Sant Joan. Martorell later recommended that Gaudí take over as architect of Sagrada Família.

Gaudí also came in contact with consummate craftsmen such as Eudald Puntí, a master of the hammer and fire who transformed iron into art. It was in Puntí's workshop that Gaudí designed one of his first projects, a display cabinet for a collection of gloves by designer Esteve Comellas. It was exhibited at the 1878 Exposition Universelle in Paris, where it deeply impressed none other than Eusebi Güell, who ultimately became one of Gaudí's most important patrons. Güell was so moved by the piece that he would not rest until he had met the artist. An appreciation for the work led to a fascination with its creator, and a lifelong friendship evolved from the meeting, which took place in Puntí's atelier.

This encounter between Gaudí and Güell was providential, not only for the commissions that resulted, significant in their scope and diversity, but also for the complete trust Güell placed in his architect, and for the freedom in which he allowed him to work. As a result of Güell's patronage, the haute bourgeoisie came to know his young protégé and his work. Gaudí became a public figure, often featured in press, despite his prickly, solitary nature. He was completely

8

devoted to his work, which was the only thing that interested him.

When the Palau Güell was under construction it was the object of much speculation and curiosity. At that time, Carrer Nou de la Rambla was one of the city's busiest locations, with the famous Edèn Concert just opposite the palace. One day Gaudí and Güell were observing the effect produced by the great wrought iron representation of the Catalan coat of arms which stood between the two entrance doors, when someone uttered a loudly pejorative remark. The owner's immediate rejoinder was, "Well, now I like it more!" The Palau Güell provoked many barbed witticisms. As the vaulted basement took shape, writer and painter Santiago Rusiñol wrote that Babylonian remains had been found there. Even the serious respected daily *La Vanguardia* printed an *innocentada*, or practical joke, on the Catalan equivalent of April Fool's Day, stating that a dungeon and lion's cage from the days of Balthasar or Nebuchadnezzar had been discovered on the site. Once the impressive building had been completed, the satirical magazine *¡Cu-cut!* published a cartoon of the facade, with the caption an exchange between two astonished citizens: "This looks like a jail," comments one. "No, it's the house of a gentleman," his friend replies.

Although Park Güell was a huge project, it was incomplete and relatively remote, thus provoking more moderate reactions from commentators and cartoonists. The satirical publication *L'Esquella*, however, observed that, while in one corner of the park a group of workmen were smashing tiles, a short distance away another team was engaged in the laborious task of reconstructing the jigsaw puzzle.

Gaudí had the courage of his convictions and refused to be put off by others' reactions. He became known for his acerbic rejoinders to comments he considered insolent, and his facial expressions reflected his disdain. The painter Porcar recalls that "his eyes resembled those of the tiger in the zoo." When a pedantic young man expressed his irritation at one of the architect's works, Gaudí replied, "I'm not doing it to please you." And when an insensitive woman asked him what the obstacles were on top of the balls that crowned Casa Calvet,

his ironic reply was, "The cross, madam, which for some is indeed an obstacle."

Needless to say, Casa Batlló also caused quite a stir. By the turn of the century, Passeig de Gràcia had become the city's grandest avenue. It was like an open-air salon where the best of Barcelona society gathered to stroll and be seen. An indication of the competitive climate of the period was the fact that Milà, on seeing the unique residence Gaudí had designed for his friend and business partner Batlló, promptly commissioned him to build an apartment building on an even more visible site. The brilliant architect was quick to take advantage of the offer, and set to work at once. The press reflected public opinion early on, as some of the cartoons show Casa Milà, or La Pedrera, surrounded by works barriers. The building was characterised as a hangar for Zeppelins, an Easter cake, and the result of an earthquake. The metal guardrails designed by Gaudí's talented collaborator Josep Maria Jujol were also the object of derision. In one cartoon an alarmed citizen asked if the twisted metal wreckage of a railway accident had been used for the project. A prospective tenant refused to rent one of the flats because he would be unable to hang out the banners for the Corpus Christi celebrations. Attacks were directed not only at the architect, but also the owner. The most pompous members of the bourgeoisie who resided in the Passeig de Gràcia snubbed the Milà family, indicating that they felt the construction of La Pedrera had caused

irreparable damage to the prestige of such a noble district. Milà also became the butt of malicious jokes concerning his second marriage to the wealthy Guardiola widow, as a *guardiola* is a moneybox in Catalan.

Prosperous members of the bourgeoisie were eager to broadcast their financial success and social position by constructing impressive buildings in the Eixample district. In *Modernisme*, architects found the freedom to break away from traditional styles and create projects that would not have been tolerated in the past. Clients sought out architects who could provide them with unique designs that would distinguish them from their neighbours and competitors. In this Güell surpassed all rivals, thanks to his ongoing collaboration with Gaudí.

Gaudí was so self-assured and committed to executing his designs without intervention from clients or bureaucrats that he ignored not only criticism but also building codes. The municipal architect Rovira i Trias refused to approve the plans for the Palau Güell; Casa Calvet was higher than regulations allowed; work on Casa Batlló was halted, as it had begun without authorisation; the dimensions of Casa Milà exceeded permitted limits, and a column at street level blocked pedestrian traffic. Unfazed by these issues, the architect responded in each case by confronting the authorities. It must be said that government officials ultimately tolerated his excesses and made exceptions to accommodate Gaudí's designs.

The people of Barcelona felt they were living in a state of grace after centuries of repression and decline. They secretly admired the controversy inspired by such a genius as Gaudí, and thrived in a city that was exploding with new life and a new freedom of expression. People

The cartoonist
Junceda, who was
harshly critical of
Modernisme,
satirised La Pedrera
in the review
En Patufet.

LA CASA-PEDRERA

— Està bé, tot m'agrada, però no us puc llogar el pis!
— Per què?
— Perquè amb aquestes baranes tan artístiques no em seria possible mai posar domassos als balcons.

from outside, however, were not prepared for such excesses. An individual from Granada who purchased a *modernista* house in Barcelona put up a sign saying: "The present owner is not responsible for this facade." Unamuno fired off insults, writing that the urban landscape of Barcelona was *fachadosa*, or facade-infested. From as far away as New York, Juan Ramón Jiménez described *modernista* Barcelona as "the victim of a Catalan architect's nightmare." Valle Inclán, indignant at the sight of the Palau Güell, described it in one of his novels as "funereal, barbarous, and Catalan."

In 1910, Clemenceau, the French Prime Minister, made a brief stopover in Barcelona on his way back to Paris from South America. He ordered a hackney carriage and asked to be driven up the Passeig de Gràcia, where he was particularly shocked by the facade of Casa Milà, La Pedrera, commenting later, "Horrible! In Barcelona they are building houses for dinosaurs and dragons!" Rusiñol had said that the only pets suitable for La Pedrera were snakes. When, in the seventies, the Parisian art dealer Maeght decided to open a gallery in Barcelona, he was tempted at first

to install it on the first floor of La Pedrera, but changed his mind when he realised that with so many curved walls and partitions it would be impossible to hang pictures for an exhibition.

Writer and cartoonist Apel·les Mestres commented that whenever a prospective client approached Gaudí, he would reply that before accepting the commission he would have to consult the Virgin Mary. Mestres added, "Unfortunately for the good name of Catalan architecture, the Virgin always told him to go ahead!" He also recounted that architect Domènech i Montaner had told him this anecdote: One day Gaudí was entrusted with the design of a pitcher. The architect racked his brains as to what the most suitable material would be until, at last, he chose wire netting!

Gaudí and the advocates and practitioners of *Modernisme* had to endure the scorn of the militants of *Noucentisme*, the early twentieth-century cultural and political movement that advocated a return to classicism and traditional Catalan values. *Noucentistes* declared their hatred of *Modernisme* claiming they felt physical discom-

In Junceda's biting cartoon published in ¡Cu-cut!, in 1910, the child exclaims, "Daddy, Daddy, I want a big Easter cake like that one!"

According to this cartoon published in L'Esquella de la Torratxa in 1912, the building would eventually become a multi-storey zeppelin garage.

fort in the presence of its works and calling for their demolition. Today it is hard to believe that action would be taken on the recommendations of such a radical group, but many important examples of an architectural style that had provided Catalan culture with its greatest splendour since Gothic times were destroyed. Even the Palau de la Música Catalana was threatened. Numerous buildings that remained standing were ignobly mutilated. In one of the most tragic cases, Arnau's sculpture, which embellished the ground-floor facade of Casa Lleó i Morera at no. 35, Passeig de Gràcia, was removed. This outrage was committed by architect Raimon Duran i Reynals, a *noucentista*, needless to say. It is difficult to believe that such destruction could be carried out by educated, cultured people; however, as Gustave Flaubert noted, ''Bad taste is the taste of the generation before,'' and *noucentistes* sought to eradicate the *Modernisme* which had preceded them.

Although he was not, strictly speaking, a *modernista*, Gaudí belonged to that generation, and suffered many of the consequences of the campaign. In fact, his radically avant-garde concepts were the object of even greater ridicule. As I have stated before, he was so committed to his artistic principles and sure of his direction that this criticism rolled off his back. He increasingly removed himself from the hubbub of worldly life, beginning in about 1911 and devoted himself body and soul to the Temple of the Sagrada Família, even living on the site during his last years. I believe that ill health precipitated this withdrawal, as in 1910 he suffered a deep depression, followed by anaemia, which rendered him defenceless against Maltese fever. His condition was so serious that he dictated his last will and testament. I suspect that he decided he had produced a sufficient body of work and could

— Ja és estrany que no la cremessin.
— Oh, és que no estava acabada.

The painter and cartoonist Martí Bas, in L'Esquella in 1937, suggested that the anarchists had not burnt down the Sagrada Família because it was still unfinished.

—¿Què vols que't digui? a n'aquet temple no li veig la punta.
—¡Y tantes que'n té!

The cartoonist Opisso, who eventually became one of Gaudí's admirers, scoffed at the Sagrada Família in the calendar published by ¡Cu-cut! in 1907.

refuse further commissions in order to concentrate on the "folly" of the Sagrada Família. In some ways, this was unfortunate, as he was mature and experienced enough to develop the technical solutions demanded by his increasingly innovative project concepts. His achievements in this regard were gaining respect. In 1915 members of the Escola d'Arquitectura de Barcelona commented on the brilliance of certain structural solutions he was applying at the time. In those academic circles his work was considered revolutionary.

Death came upon Gaudí suddenly. One afternoon he was walking, as was his custom, to the Church of Sant Felip Neri to pray when he was run over by a tram while crossing the Granvia near Carrer Bailèn. Because of his ragged

appearance, he was not recognised or given the emergency treatment he required. He died three days later in the Hospital de la Santa Creu. He was buried in the Sagrada Família, the church to which he had devoted no fewer than forty-three years of his life.

Shortly after the outbreak of the Civil War in 1936, *L'Esquella* published a pencil drawing by Martí Bas, featuring the following exchange between two citizens of Barcelona: One declares himself to be astonished to see that the Sagrada Família had not fallen victim to revolutionary arsonists; the other replies, "Oh, that's because it hasn't been finished." Humour aside, I very much fear that some would have been overjoyed to witness the destruction of such an unorthodox work of architecture. Apart from Güell, his artistic collaborators, and a few critics such as Ràfols or Pujols, I feel that none of his contemporaries believed in Gaudí's genius. At best he was respected as an imaginative eccentric. When his work was exhibited in the Grand Palais in Paris in 1910 Gaudí was praised but misunderstood for both aesthetic and religious reasons. Some of the works shown were exhibited the following year at the first Salón de la Arquitectura in the Retiro, Madrid, organised by the Associació d'Arquitectes de Catalunya. Salvador Dalí deserves recognition as Gaudí's first staunch defender; he perceived the scope and rarity of the architect's genius as no one had before. Thanks to Dalí, Surrealists such as Breton, Crevel, and Cocteau became aware of his work and spread the word throughout the most revolutionary international cultural circles. The 1929 Barcelona World Exposition also provided travellers and writers, including Evelyn Waugh, with the opportunity to marvel at Gaudí's work. His first champion among architects was, perhaps, Le Corbusier, whose reputation in avant-garde circles undoubtedly contributed to a just appraisal of the Catalan's work.

Nonetheless, international awareness of Gaudí's genius did not come until 1952, when American historian George R. Collins presented a major exhibition of his work in New York. The Japanese have since expressed a boundless passion and fascination for Gaudí. Ironically, recognition of Gaudí's contributions to the field of architecture have led to a re-evaluation in recent years of the merits of *Modernisme*, a movement with which he was only loosely associated. Recognition on a more popular level of both Gaudí and the *Modernistes* came with the 1992 Olympic Games in Barcelona. Today, Gaudí's work is known and admired all over the world, and the image of Barcelona is inextricably linked to his work.

Early Works

The earliest of Gaudí's extant works are the street lamps he designed in 1878 for the Plaça Reial. Two examples of the six-branched version were erected on the occasion of the Mercè festivities that year. The cast iron and bronze lamp posts stand on stone pedestals, and are crowned with helmets evoking the god Mercury. In the Plaça Palau a pair of three-branched lamps, with inverted crowns replacing the helmets, have flanked the side entrance to the Civil Governor's Palace since 1889. At one time a civil governor ordered the removal of the crowns, as he perceived their inversion as an attack against the monarchy; luckily, that action was never taken. The helmet was not a new element for Gaudí, as he had used it some years earlier to top the entrance gates to the Parc de la Ciutadella. He collaborated on that project as an assistant to Josep Fontserè, who was responsible for the design and execution of the gardens. Gaudí also designed elements of the waterfall and the stone balustrade around the monument to Aribau.

Between 1879 and 1881 he worked on what is today the Parish Church of Sant Pacià at no. 27, Carrer de les Monges, in the Sant Andreu de Palomar district, designing the flooring, altar, and tabernacle. The latter two were destroyed by fire during the Setmana Tràgica, or Tragic Week, riots of 1909. The design he made for the floor was based on the Roman mosaic technique.

Cast-iron and bronze lamppost, crowned by a helmet symbolising the god Mercury, in the Plaça Reial.

Inventory of No Longer Existing Works in Barcelona

Fortunately, only lesser Barcelona works were destroyed. Here follows the list of the most interesting:

1879

Decoration of the Farmàcia Gibert, on the corner of Plaça de Catalunya and Fontanella

1902

Part of the interior decor of Bar Torino, on Passeig de Gràcia/Gran Via

1904

Doorway for the Chalet Graner, Carrer de la Immaculada, 44–46

Tallers Badia, industrial nave, Carrer Nàpols, 278

Part of the interior decor of the Sala Mercè, La Rambla, 122

The standard for the Locksmiths Guild

Inventory of the Most Important Extant Projects Outside Barcelona

1883–1885

Comillas: El Capricho

1887–1893

Astorga: The Episcopal Palace

1891–1892

León: La Casa de los Botines

1903–1914

Palma de Mallorca: restoration of the Cathedral

1.
Comillas
El Capricho

2.
Astorga
The Episcopal Palace

3.
León
Casa de los Botines

4.
Palma de Mallorca
Restoration of the
Cathedral

PARC DEL
CASTELL DE
L'ORENETA

RONDA DE DALT

**Bellesguard,
la Casa Figueras**

RONDA DE DALT

RONDA DE DALT

C. DE DANTE ALIGHIERI

PG. DE LA REINA ELISENDA

VIA AUGUSTA

AV. DEL TIBIDABO

PARC DE
LA CREUETA
DEL COLL

C. DEL LLOBREGÓS

RAMBLA DEL CARMEL

AV. DE PEDRALBES

PG. DE LA BONANOVA

PG. DE SANT GERVASI

PL. DE LA
BONANOVA

C. DE BALMES

AV. DE LA REPÚBLICA ARGENTINA

AV. 3 DE L' HOSPITAL MILITAR

TURÓ DEL
PUTGET

PARK
GÜELL

PARC DEL
CARMEL

**Pavellons
Palau Reial Finca Güell**
DE PEDRALBES

PARC DEL
PALAU REIAL

VIA AUGUSTA

**Col·legi de
les Teresianes**

RONDA DEL GENERAL MITRE

PARC DE
MONTEROLS

Parc Güell

**Porta de la
finca Miralles**

C. DE GANDUXER

PL. DE
LESSEPS

PARC DEL
GUINARDÓ

GRAN VIA DE CARLES III

AV. DE SARRIÀ

TRAVESSERA DE DALT

AV. DE PEDRALBES

AV. DIAGONAL

VIA AUGUSTA

AV. DEL PRÍNCEP D'ASTÚRIES

Casa Vicens

C. DE L'ESCORIAL

PARC DE
LES AIGÜES

TRAV. DE LES CORTS

TURÓ
PARC

C. DE MUNTANER

C. DE BALMES

C. DE GRAN DE GRÀCIA

C. DEL TORRENT DE L'OLLA

C. DE PI I MARGALL

RONDA DEL GUINARDÓ

C. DE BRASIL

AV. DE MADRID

PL. DE
LES CORTS

PL. DE
FRANCESC
MACIÀ

TRAVESSERA DE GRÀCIA

C. DE SANT ANTONI MARIA CLARET

HOSPITAL DE
LA SANTA CREU
I SANT PAU

C. DE NUMÀNCIA

C. DE JOSEP TARRADELLAS

C. DE LONDRES

C. D'ARIBAU

AV. DIAGONAL

C. DE CÒRSEGA

PL. DELS
PAÏSOS
CATALANS

C. DE CÒRSEGA

C. DE PARÍS

C. DEL ROSSELLÓ

AV. DE GAUDÍ

C. DE SANTS

PARC DE
L'ESPANYA
INDUSTRIAL

C. D'ENTENÇA

C. DE PROVENÇA

C. DEL COMTE D'URGELL

C. DE BALMES

PG. DE GRÀCIA

**Casa Milà,
La Pedrera**

PL. MOSSEN JACINT
VERDAGUER

C. DE SARDENYA

**Temple de la
Sagrada Família**

C. DE TARRAGONA

AV. DE ROMA

C. DE MALLORCA

C. DE VALÈNCIA

PG. DE SANT JOAN

AV. DIAGONAL

C. DE CARTAGENA

PARC DE
JOAN MIRÓ
(ESCORXADOR)

C. D'ARAGÓ

Casa Batlló

C. DE ROGER DE FLOR

C. DEL CONSELL DE CENT

C. DE LA DIPUTACIÓ

PL. DE
TETUAN

PL. DE LES
GLÒRIES
CATALANES

PL.
D'ESPANYA

GRAN VIA DE LES CORTS CATALANES

C. DE CASP

C. D'ÀLABA

C. DE SEPÚLVEDA

C. DE PELAI

Casa Calvet

AV. MISTRAL

RONDA DE SANT ANTONI

PL. DE
CATALUNYA

RONDA DE SANT PERE

C. D'AUSIÀS MARC

PARC DE
L'ESTACIÓ
DEL NORD

AV. MERIDIANA

C. DELS ALMOGÀVERS

C. DE LLEIDA

RONDA DE SANT PAU

VIA LAIETANA

C. DE PERE IV

AV. DEL PARAL·LEL

LA RAMBLA

C. DE PUJADES

AV. DE L'ESTADI

C. DE SANT PAU

C. DE FERRAN

C. DE LA PRINCESA

PG. PICASSO

PARC
DE LA
CIUTADELLA

C. DE LA MARINA

C. DE LLULL

C. NOU DE LA RAMBLA

**Fanals de la
Plaça Reial**

Palau Güell

**Fanals del
Govern Civil**

PG. DE COLOM

AV. D'ICÀRIA

MONTJUÏC

RONDA DEL LITORAL

RONDA DEL LITORAL

MEDITERRANEAN SEA

The Works: Illustrations and Comentaries

Casa Vicens

1878–1888

Carrer de les Carolines, 18–24
Gràcia District

*Detail of the palmetto-leaf fence
on the principal facade.*

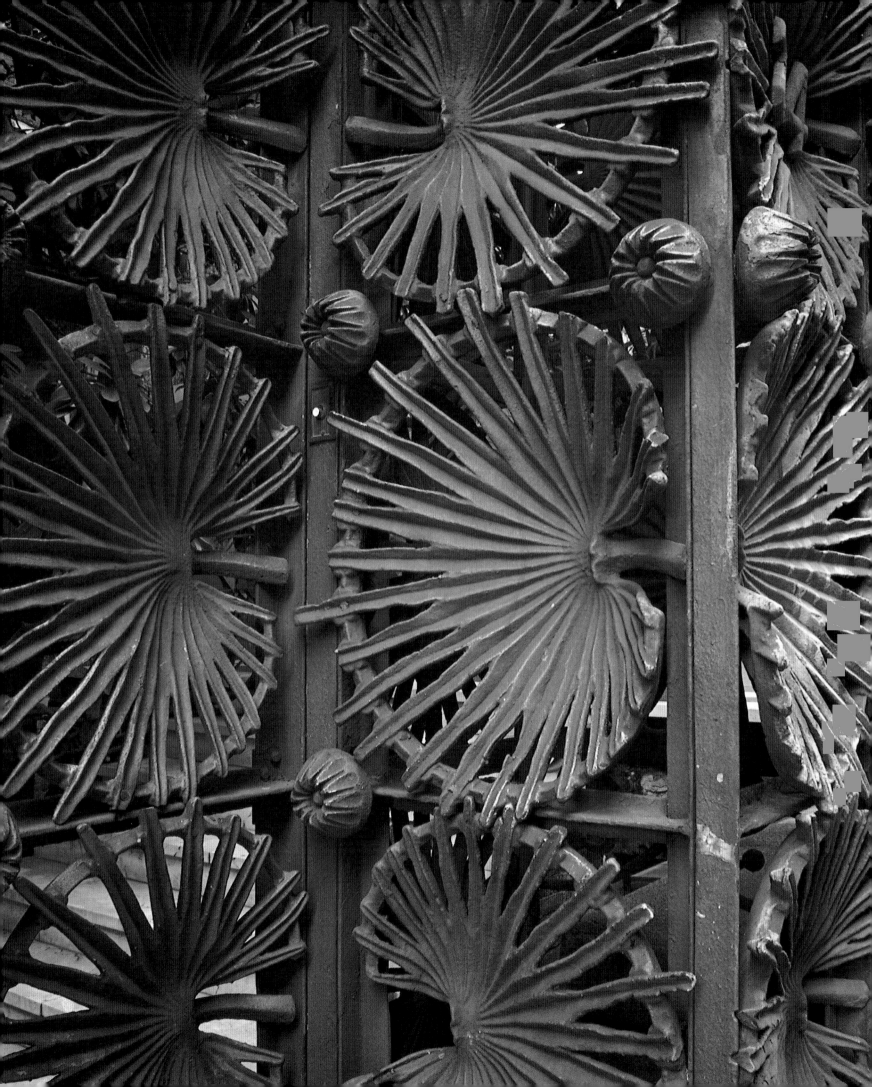

Casa Vicens

In 1878, Manuel Vicens Montaner commissioned Gaudí to design a house and garden for the site he had purchased at no. 24, Carrer de les Carolines, in the Gràcia district. The majority of the project was completed between 1883 and 1885, with details added until 1888. Vicens was a ceramic tile manufacturer, a metier to which Gaudí paid homage by incorporating this material in his design.

The visual impact of Casa Vicens is dramatic. The bold formal composition, particularly of the

View from Carrer de les Carolines.
Opposite: The intricate tile and ironwork decoration on the facade.

arcaded upper floors rising to the rooftop's asymmetrical ensemble of turrets and sloping planes, contributes to the forceful personality of the house. No less potent is Gaudí's use of polychromy. A dazzling pattern of colourful tiles contrasts with bands of exposed brickwork and rubble, emphasising certain structural elements and showing a Moorish or *mudéjar* influence. Architect and historian Ignasi de Solà-Morales is among those who see Mediterranean and Arab traditions in this building technique. Gaudí integrated tiles, stone, brick, and iron with true mastery. These materials come together in a rich, complex dialogue harmoniously orchestrated by the architect.

While the exterior impresses with its bold personality, the interior is characterised by ornamentation which leaves no corner untouched, resulting in a wholly integrated work. This approach would become characteristic of Gaudí's oeuvre. Each interior space is a world unto itself, with its own distinct ambience. The smoking room, for example, with its honeycombed ceiling, shows a clear Moorish influence. Architectural historian Joan Bassegoda detects traces of a freely interpreted Far Eastern influence in such details as the blinds originally used on the balcony. The profuse decoration and perfect finishes throughout the house are the work of experienced craftsmen; painter Josep Torrescassana and sculptor Antoni Riba were among the artists who contributed to the project under Gaudí's direction.

Over time, urban development, including the widening of the street, led to alterations in

The profusion of
tile reflects the
professional interests
of the client.

The facade is
characterised by
a vertical rhythm
emphasised by the
tile patterns.

On both interior and exterior both pattern and shape reflect a Moorish influence.

The smoking room.

Casa Vicens and its site as originally conceived; fortunately, none were too significant. Those undertaken by the architect Joan B. de Serra Martínez in 1925–26 were actually supervised by Gaudí. At that time the wall and railing that enclosed the property were removed. Fragments of the railing are preserved in the Park Güell, the Museu Güell, and the school of the same name. In 1946 part of the garden was sold for the development of a block of flats, and in 1962 a small temple on the grounds dedicated to Santa Rita was razed for the construction of additional flats. Casa Vicens was awarded the prestigious annual Barcelona City Hall Prize in 1927.

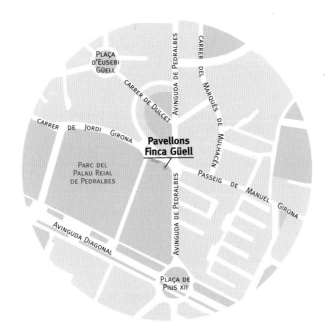

PLAÇA D'EUSEBI GÜELL
CARRER DE DULCET
AVINGUDA DE PEDRALBES
CARRER DEL MARQUÈS DE MULHACÉN
CARRER DE JORDI GIRONA
Pavellons Finca Güell
PARC DEL PALAU REIAL DE PEDRALBES
PASSEIG DE MANUEL GIRONA
AVINGUDA DE PEDRALBES
AVINGUDA DIAGONAL
PLAÇA DE PIUS XII

The Güell Estate Pavilions
1884–1887

Avinguda de Pedralbes, 7
Carrer de Manuel Girona
Sarrià / Sant Gervasi District

Detail of the exterior wall
of the caretaker's lodge.

The Güell
Estate Pavilions

In the mid-nineteenth century, Joan Güell i Ferrer, a prominent textile manufacturer, purchased two extensive estates in the Les Corts district of Barcelona: Can Feliu and Torre Baldiró. In 1883 his son and heir, Eusebi Güell i Bacigalupi, extended the property considerably by acquiring the adjoining estate known as Can Cuyàs de la Riera. Eusebi Güell was married to a daughter

View of the caretaker's lodge from Avinguda de Pedralbes.

of the Marqués de Comillas, a supporter of the arts, for whom Gaudí designed a chapel pew in 1878. Güell became aware of Gaudí's work through his father-in-law and was particularly impressed with his designs for the 1878 Exposition Universelle in Paris.

Güell, who was to become Gaudí's most important patron, approached Gaudí in 1884 to work on the estate. The commission originally included a wall marking the property boundaries, three entrance gates, an arbour and fountain, and modifications to the residence. Only the main gate, flanked by a caretaker's lodge and coach house with stables, remains. An imposing dragon of beaten iron surmounts the gate. As the mythological jealous keeper of the enchanted garden of the Hesperides, he receives visitors with wide-open jaws. The gate is composed of cast iron plates, each stamped with a rose, and the gatepost is crowned by an antimony orange tree featuring the owner's initial ''G'' framed by wild roses. The structure is a spectacular example of *modernista*, or Catalan art nouveau, design.

To the left stands the octagonal caretaker's lodge, and to the right the stable and coach house, which now contain the offices of the Càtedra Gaudí (the Gaudí Chair of Architecture at Barcelona University, established in 1956). Gaudí used parabolic vaults and arches to create the interior space of the latter, which is striking in its structural simplicity and decorative restraint.

In the early 1920s, Eusebi Güell's son Joan Antoní turned over part of the estate to the royal family of Spain for their residence in Barcelona. Two of the gates ceased to have any purpose after the estate was divided. One currently stands beside the biology building and the other (demolished and reconstructed) is located near the chemistry building of Barcelona University, which now occupies most of what was once the Güell estate. In 1983, the fountain that was part of the original commission was found intact beneath a thick blanket of vegetation where the royal gardens had been laid out.

The stables

The gateposts are crowned with elaborate ornament.

The dragon gate, perhaps the most spectacular wrought-iron sculpture of Modernisme.

Palau Güell

1885–1890

Carrer Nou de la Rambla, 3–5
Ciutat Vella District

*Detail of the coffered ceiling in the
living and dining room.*

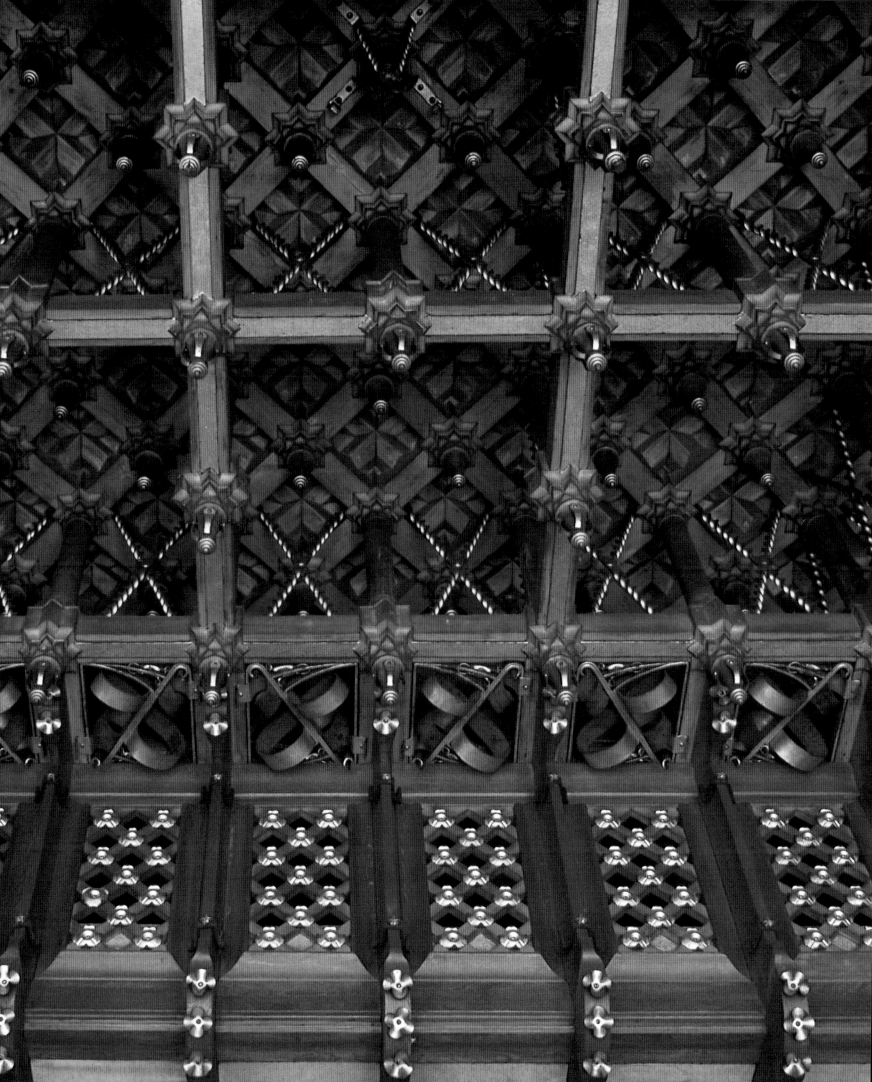

Palau Güell

Eusebi Güell was so pleased with Gaudí's work on his estate that he engaged the architect to design a town house. The site was located not in the *Eixample*, the city extension laid out on the grid system by Ildefons Cerdà where many aristocrats were building their houses at this time, but on the Rambla, where the Güell family had traditionally resided. When he inherited the family's town house from his father, along with an adjacent property at no. 5, Carrer Nou, Güell asked Gaudí to build him a mansion which would complement the existing house and be linked to it through a gallery connecting at the rear. The new palace was conceived as a venue for social gatherings and as a contemporary symbol of the Güell family's status.

Palau Güell was Gaudí's largest commission to date and highly significant for both architect and patron. Eusebi Güell placed his trust in an avant-garde architect not only because he was sympathetic to progressive, modern art, but also because he sought to differentiate himself from other prominent members of the aristocracy and bourgeoisie. His selection of Gaudí was also important to the emerging Catalan art nouveau movement known as *Modernisme*, with which Gaudí was loosely associated. By commissioning a large residence on a conspicuous site in Barcelona from an architect whom he knew would produce a highly individualistic design, Güell signaled his determination to embark on an architectural adventure and make his mark on the cityscape. He knew Gaudí would produce an exceptional and unorthodox work, one that would distinguish him as a patron.

Gaudí began the project in 1885 and construction work was completed in 1889, although the complex interior decoration was not satisfactorily resolved until the following year. The facade overlooking Carrer Nou de la Rambla is of exceptional quality, with all the solemnity the brief

The principal facade, made of Garraf stone from Güell's quarries.

The wrought-iron entrance gates incorporate Güell's initials. Between them is an elaborate sculptural rendition of the Catalan coat of arms.

required. It certainly does not reflect the deliberate break from traditional forms shown in later works by the architect, such as Casa Batlló or La Pedrera. The slightly asymmetrical facade is constructed of Garraf stone, extracted from Güell's own quarries on the precipitous coast near Sitges. The pattern of fenestration gives the surface a discreet horizontality. Detailed with striking decorative elements, the composition is supremely elegant, one in which some have suggested a relationship with Venetian palazzos. The pair of parabolic entrance arches signals the extensive use of this structural element throughout the interior. Each gate has a densely entangled *modernista* design, with the patron's initials "E" in one and "G" in the other. Between the gates is a spectacular cylinder depicting the Catalan coat of arms, intricately crafted of wrought iron. Gaudí achieved a dramatic sculptural volume in the striped *senyera*, or Catalan flag, surmounted by helmet and eaglet.

In the interior spaces, Gaudí's highly individual approach and rejection of precedent is evident in every detail. The main entrance leads down to the basement, as well as up to the formal rooms of the palace. The stables were located below, reached by a spiral ramp, and the space is surprisingly beautiful. Through the use of humble materials such as brick and tile, Gaudí was able to attain an unwonted expressiveness. The broad, unadorned columns preside with aplomb over this unique complex.

One level up from the main entrance, a cluster of salons is arranged around a central hall, which measures nine metres in length and almost twenty metres high. This great hall, the center of all the life of the palace, is reminiscent of the interior open patios so characteristic of Mediterranean architecture. A star-studded celestial dome crowns the space, evoking the distant firmament. The great parabolic arch forming the dome is the largest of many found throughout the interior. The dome is actually a double form: a parabolic vault inside, and a sculptural needle on the roof outside, crowned by a lightning rod and weather vane. The space is enriched by an interplay of filtered light that endows each of the decorative elements with astonishingly changeable tones and colours.

A stone forest of columns encloses this magical central space. Highly diverse in both form and function, displaying an extraordinary quality of texture and finish, the columns total 127, including one which acts as a kind of extra verse. Railings and recessed spaces around the great salon concealed musicians from view on concert evenings. Unfortunately, the organ pipes disappeared when the palace was occupied during the Civil War. One of the spaces was designated as a chapel for private family worship. Painted by Aleix Clapés, the chapel originally contained a sculpture of the Virgin by Joan Flotats, which was destroyed in 1936. Canvases painted by Clapés also hang on nearby walls.

Many others contributed to the superb interior decoration of the palace, including ironworkers Joan Oños, Salvador Gabarrós, and Badía Hermanos; carpenter Julià Soley; joiner Eudald Puntí; marble cutters Ventura Hermanos; decorator Antoni Oliva; and architect Camil Oliveras, who also worked as a decorator. Gaudí had by now become a consummate orchestra conductor, able to draw the best from each of the artists and craftsmen working under his baton.

Dominating the rear facade is a gallery that links the two buldings. An awning of wooden shutters filters the light through the gallery windows.

He brought their individual talents together masterfully in the expression of his artistic vision.

The rear facade maintains a dialogue with the street facade, in terms of both the spirit of the project and the materials employed. I would venture to observe that the rear facade and gallery are more deliberately innovative than the entrance. Barcelona is a city rich in galleries, and that of the Palau Güell is outstanding among them. One of its surprising aspects is its relative opacity. The textures and colours of wood, iron, and glazed ceramic are beautifully integrated, and the awning composed of timber slats contributes to the gallery's strong visual impact.

Gaudí finished off this astonishing work with an unexpected surprise, transforming a utilitarian complex of chimneys and ventilators into an imaginative sculptural paradise that heralded the coming century of avant-garde art. The pieces assert their striking presence through the innovative use of materials and the visual impact of the polychrome facing. There are no less than twenty sculptures surrounding the spire that corresponds to the interior dome of the central salon. Some pieces are constructed of such humble materials as brick or stucco. Others have been clad in ceramic fragments. Gaudí made masterful use of a traditional Catalan technique, *trencadís de ceràmica*, or broken ceramic fragments. It was an inexpensive, colourful, and durable means of covering a curved surface. Through his sensitivity, the architect achieved aesthetic results which raised the technique to the category of art. By exploring the expressive possibilities of texture, form, and colour in such detail in these rooftop sculptures, Gaudí demonstrated that for him, as the poet Salvat-Papasseit said, "*Res no és mesqui* (Nothing is insignificant)." This rooftop sculpture garden anticipated what he would later attain on a more ambitious scale at La Pedrera.

Some of the chimneys were left unfinished by Gaudí. In 1994, Antonio González Moreno-Navarro, the architect responsible for historic

The principal public and family rooms open onto the great hall.

The rich decorative
scheme, orchestrated
by Gaudi, included
ironwork, marble,
and elaborate joinery.

View into the central hall from the grand salon.

preservation at the Barcelona County Council, which owns the palace, invited a number of artists and architects to face the pieces using the *trencadís de ceràmica* technique. The result is highly satisfactory, in that there is no trace of imitation and the designs are innovative within the parameters of the original concept.

In 1906, Eusebi Güell gave up the palace as his private residence and, in an act of faith and in order to serve as an example, went to live in the great urban adventure which, under Gaudí's influence, he had undertaken at Park Güell. Immediately after the Civil War, Catalonia was on the brink of losing the palace; an American millionaire was negotiating with the Güell family

not only for the purchase of this masterpiece, but, worse still, its transportation stone-by-stone across the Atlantic. This and other perils were definitively staved off when in 1954 the County Council, by then the owners, resolved to transform the building into the Museum of the Theatrical Arts. This new use not only dignified the palace, which can now be visited, but led to its restoration by Antonio González, an architect sensitive to the nuances of historic preservation.

Of all the works by Gaudí, Palau Güell is among the best preserved, and it still has the power to evoke its original atmosphere. Few buildings can match the intensity of its visual impact, particularly in the interior spaces.

Carrer de Pau Alcover
Carrer de Ganduxer
Carrer dels Vergós
Col·legi de les Teresianes
Carrer de Mandri
Carrer de les Escoles Pies
Carrer del Milanesat
Carrer d'Alacant
Via Augusta
Ronda del General Mitre
Carrer de Vico
Carrer de Ganduxer
Carrer de Modolell

The Teresianes School

1889–1894

Carrer de Ganduxer, 95–105
Sarrià / Sant Gervasi District

Detail of the arches in the gallery.

The Teresianes School

In 1889, Gaudí received a visit from Father Enric d'Ossó i Cervelló, founder of the Companyia de Santa Teresa, an institution devoted to girls' education. The priest proposed that Gaudí take on the design of his religious institution, a project that had been started the previous year by another architect. The site was located in what was then the township of Sant Gervasi de Cassoles, now Carrer de Ganduxer in the Barcelona district of Sant Gervasi. Father d'Ossó's reasons for changing direction midstream are unknown. As for Gaudí's interest in taking up a project with a very restricted budget and tight deadline that was already under construction, I suspect that he was intrigued by his prospective client, a man of the church who, like himself, was from Tarragona. He would also have been attracted to the idea of building a religious school. Further, I would contend that Gaudí liked the challenge of the project's parameters. In any case, he began work at once.

The building's design is a testament to the architect's amazing versatility, in that he was able to rein in his unorthodox imagination, resisting the temptation to embark on an ornate decorative adventure in order to adhere to the budget and respect the function of

Wrought-iron entrance gate.

The integration of
simple materials into a
rigorous geometry and bold
rhythm creates an
imposing facade.

the school. Gaudí adapted the design to the prosaic needs of his client, and the result is magnificent.

The Teresianes School is characterised by the sobriety of its form and the austerity of its interior. Gaudí restricted himself to building smooth walls of brick and rubble, attaining maximum expression through the repetition of the same module along the sixty metres of facade. Despite such a minimalist concept, the overall effect created by the parabolic and non-parabolic windows, the curtain wall of shutters flush with the surface, crenellations, and pinnacles is attractive and imposing. A chiaroscuro counterpoint subtly plays across the facade.

Inside, Gaudí took this minimalism a step further, composing a series of magical spaces. Through an interior patio, natural light is distributed throughout. The high and narrow parabolic arches of surrounding cloisters, unadorned by decorative elements, create a dramatic effect, seductive in their simplicity.

Needless to say, relations between two such obstinate individuals as Gaudí and d'Ossó were fragile in the extreme. When the school's founder complained of the cost of some materials, Gaudí told him to go to the devil, as the building process was the architect's responsibility. Despite these tensions and the scant resources, the school was opened in 1890, and work continued until 1894.

Brickwork patterns
dominate the facade,
enclosing panels of
rubble stone and
ceramic details.

Simple brickwork frames the elaborate joinery of a door.

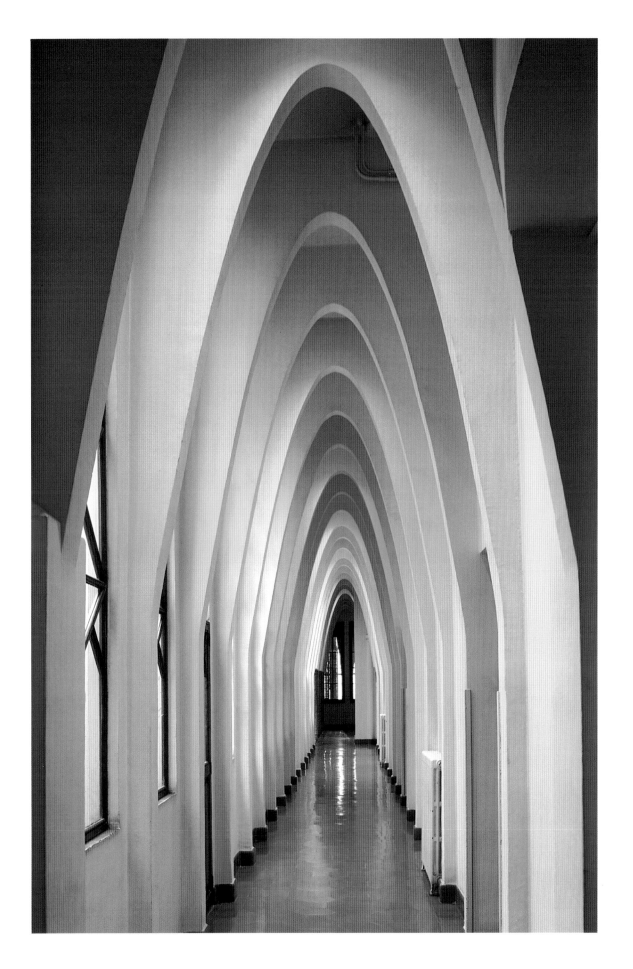

Slender parabolic arches transofrm the gallery into a space of awesome simplicity.

Above: The central vestibule.

Right: A simple twist gives a brick column sculptural form.

Opposite: The cloister opens onto an interior court.

Casa Calvet

1898–1900

Carrer de Casp, 48
L'Eixample District

*Detail of tiles lining the entrance
hall and stairwell.*

Casa Calvet

In 1898, the widow of textile manufacturer Pere Màrtir Calvet i Carbonell commissioned Gaudí to design a building for both residential and business use at no. 48, Carrer de Casp. Although the site was undistinguished, it was located in the heart of the Eixample district, where the city's haute bourgeoisie lived at the time. Although Casa Calvet is recognisable as a work of *Modernisme*, it is perhaps the architect's most conventional and least audacious work. In view of his uncompromising personality, it is hard to imagine that he would have succumbed to pressure from his client to produce an unobtrusive yet extremely high quality facade, as some would have us believe. Gaudí's reasons for making these design decisions are unknown.

The facade, consisting entirely of rough-hewn ashlar stone, is surprising in that it was the only instance in which Gaudí cultivated symmetry, which he considered an exercise in repetition. The rhythm between solid and void, smooth stone and ornamentation, seems very balanced and functional. The gallery at ground level is the facade's most outstanding feature, a daring combination of wrought iron and stone in which decorative historical elements such as a cypress, an olive tree, horns of plenty, and the Catalan coat of arms can be discerned. At the roof line, a double gable breaks the predominantly linear arrangement. Punctuating these gables are the building's most original balconies, complete with winches to hoist furniture. They anticipate the design of the Casa Batlló balconies a few years later. Crowning the facade are a number of decorative elements which have symbolic significance for the family. Sant Pere Màrtir, a reference to the owner's father, Sant Genís Notari, and Sant Genís Còmic are the patron saints of Vilassar, Calvet's home town. Further such details include columns sculpted in the form of stacked bobbins, referring to the family business, and the mushrooms above the gallery balustrade which pay tribute to the patriarch's favourite hobby.

The vestibule is an impressive complex, beginning with the large, cross-shaped wrought iron door knockers that strike a bedbug, considered at the time to be the embodiment of evil. The parapet tiling, well-turned spiral columns, and

The symmetrical facade is crowned by an undulating roofline punctuated with sculpture.

painted ceiling are all magnificent examples of Gaudí's prowess as a designer. No detail—not even the peepholes and doorknobs—escaped his attention.

For his client's offices the architect designed formidable pieces of organic, sensually curvilinear oak furniture, which was manufactured by the highly respected firm Casas & Bardès. Some of this furniture can now be admired in the Gaudí Museum-House. It is only relatively recently, however, that we have been able to savour the space for which these pieces were designed: the owner's offices, which occupied the entire ground floor of the building. This exquisite space, magnificently detailed by Gaudí, was preserved intact. Not long ago it became the Restaurant Casa Calvet, and the proprietors were respectful of the original design in their conversion. Outstanding elements include the lobby benches, the double benches against the wall, and the partitions separating different areas of the original office, all of which are dovetailed, fitted together without a single nail. Fascinating details from another period remain, such as the list of payments which figures on the outer frame of one of the private room doors. Although certain elements had to be reproduced in the new construction, it is nonetheless thrilling to experience a fully operational work by Gaudí and discover the absolute modernity of certain elements.

The wrought-iron
cage of the elevator
dominates the
richly decorated
entrance hall.

Left and following pages: Decorative details in the entrance hall and stairwell demonstrate the high level of design and craftsmanship.

The elaborate wrought-iron door knocker and specially designed hardware.

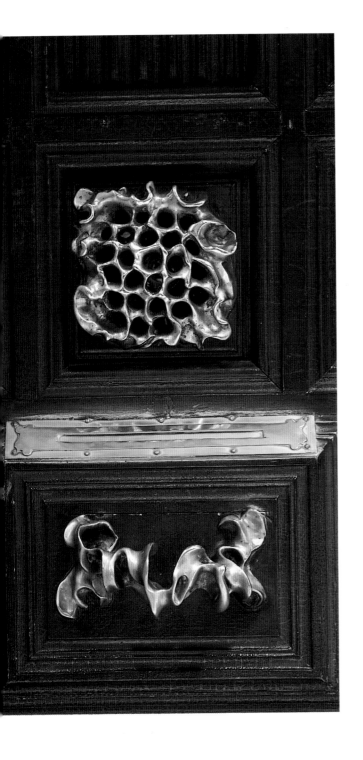

Original oak
partitions and brass
light fixtures have
been preserved in the
Restaurant Casa
Calvet, formerly the
family offices.

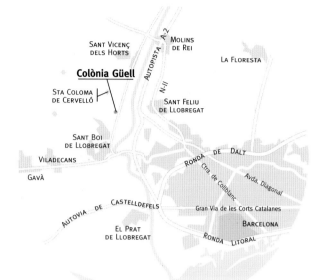

The Colònia Güell Crypt
1898–1915

Santa Coloma de Cervelló

Detail of the colourful ceramic and glass decoration above the entrance.

The Colònia Güell Crypt

The Colònia Güell crypt is the only work featured in this volume that stands outside Barcelona; however, by virtue of its proximity to the city (Santa Coloma de Cervelló is only fifteen kilometres away), the fact that it was commissioned by Gaudí's greatest patron, and its importance to the evolution of the architect's work, the crypt deserves to be included in this itinerary.

Eusebi Güell owned about thirty hectares of land on the outskirts of Barcelona on which he resolved to develop a workers' settlement for the textile factories already established there. Perhaps influenced by similar communities he had observed on frequent trips to England, Güell created an industrial/residential estate which included factories and houses, sports fields, cooperatives, and theatres. Architects Francesc Berenguer and Joan Rubió i Bellver were responsible for many of the original structures. In 1898, when it was becoming clear that the existing church was inadequate for the growing population, Güell approached Gaudí to design a new one. Construction did not begin until 1908, and the chapel was not consecrated until 1915. At that time only the crypt was completed, and the rest of the project would never be finished.

In order to explain why ten years passed between the original commission and the laying of the foundation stone, it is necessary to understand that the architect was determined to break

The church built by Gaudí for Güell's industrial/residential complex.

The complex is subtly integrated into its natural surroundings, an approach that characterises much of Gaudí's mature work.

The entrance door with the decorative panel of ceramics and glass above.

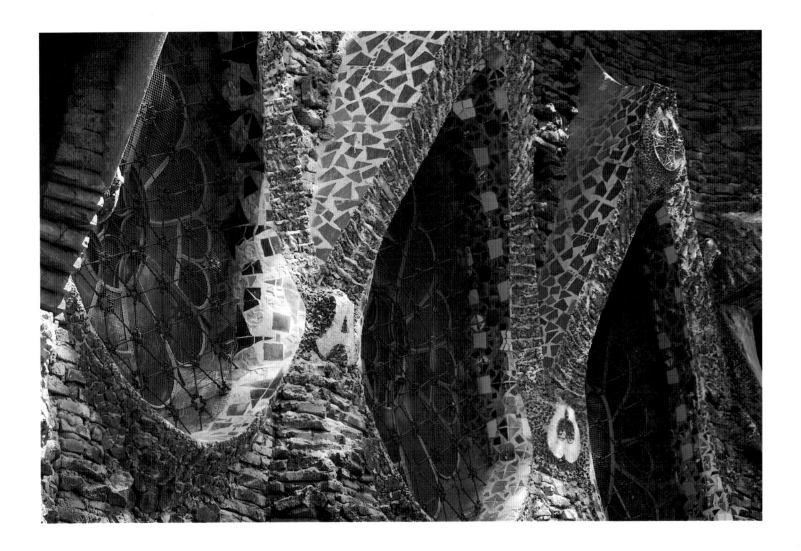

from all precedent to create a boldly innovative and brilliant work. For the first time in his career, Gaudí wanted structure alone to be the essence of his design. Consequently, he developed an approach in which the empirical study of loads and stresses replaced more traditional mathematical formulas in the determination of structural systems. To this end, he invented a curious and highly complex funicular model in which ropes and weights visually represented the behaviour of forces. Gaudí specialist and architect Joan Bassegoda i Nonell has most clearly explained this complicated process: "The most astonishing aspect of this structure was its calculation system, based on the physical properties of ropes which, made taut by the weight of bags containing buckshot, adopted a form which, when inverted, corresponded to the pressure line of a compressed arch loaded with weights proportional to those of the bags. In this way, by determining the loads and suspending bags with proportional weights from a series of strings, the ideal form of the structure was attained without recourse to the application of mathematical calculations." It is not surprising that such a revolutionary system was beset by considerable difficulties. The most

The window grilles were fashioned from knitting needles; ceramic fragments enhance the window surrounds.

85

An intricate web of
arches forms the
ceiling of the porch.

Light filtered through skylights and stained-glass windows enriches the sanctuary.

obvious of these is that as soon as any of the weights were varied, an imbalance was created in a series of bags, which then had to be re-balanced. The more central the weight being changed, the greater the chain reaction of imbalance requiring a series of corrections. The system was primitive and delicate, and mastery came only through endless experimentation. This is one reason why the design evolved so slowly and the project took so long to execute. I believe, also, that Gaudí needed time to clarify his ideas, as he was breaking entirely new ground in terms of his creative process and the expression of his artistic vision.

Once overall balance had been achieved, the maze of rope, strings, and weighted bags was photographed by sculptor Vicente Villarrubias. When the photographs were developed and turned upside down they revealed the way the forms were to be constructed. Gaudí then painted the ornamental details directly onto the photographs, following the structural lines created by the hanging weights.

An irregular plan responding to the contours of the site would become the basis for many of Gaudí's mature works. The cavernous crypt space and colonnaded porch rise organically in a small pine wood. While structural elements are usually disguised, here they are exaggerated and exposed so that they become the focal point. Such an aesthetic forced the architect to adopt a design vocabulary that acquired the crudeness of primitive gestures. It is in this context that we pay tribute to a simple structure of unprecedented beauty. Its twisting arches, ribbed vaults, and leaning columns signal Gaudí's highly personal, unorthodox vision. The four basalt columns in the nave, each roughly hewn from three stones marking base, shaft, and capital,

The nave and central altar.

Rough-hewn brick contrasts with the delicacy of stained glass.

are dramatic expressions of structure. While the pervasive atmosphere is cave-like, and natural light does not uniformly bathe the interior, the architect enhanced the light that does enter by filtering it through panes of coloured glass. This light, measured and of extraordinary quality, gives the interior a magical quality.

Refusing to consider any material unworthy, Gaudí even incorporated items recovered from trash into his design. The window grilles, for example, are ingeniously fashioned from old knitting needles. Gaudí's assistant Josep Maria Jujol designed the left-hand and central altars, of which only the shrine remains. The right-hand altar was the work of architect Isidre Puig Boada. The pews are crafted of iron and wood, and were designed particularly for this space.

Whenever I am inside this crypt, I am overcome by the sensation that everything is in motion, and that this dynamism is the result both of a deliberate aesthetic and the impression that each element has been endowed with an inner life and a voice with which it can forcefully express itself. In the Colònia Güell crypt we have evidence that it is not necessarily monumentality which makes art great or provides its impact. Here, there is an emotional intensity that gives the structure its power.

Park Güell

1900–1914

Carrer d'Olot
Gràcia District

*Detail of the trencadis de ceràmica designed for the Hall of the
Hundred Columns by Gaudi's collaborator Josep Maria Jujol.*

Park Güell

It was at the turn of the century that Eusebi Güell assigned Gaudí to this ambitious, innovative project; his work continued until 1914. Güell travelled to England often, and, although there is no documentary evidence to support this theory, some believe he was inspired by the garden suburbs that had begun to spring up there. Others insist that he was much influenced by

Inside the entrance gate a sinuous double staircase leads up the the Hall of the Hundred Columns.

View from the
plaza on the roof of
the Hall of the
Hundred Columns.

a stay in Nîmes. It must be stressed that Güell never intended the park to be anything but a private residential estate. The Barcelona industrialist had already built a utopian workers' community at his textile complex in Santa Coloma de Cervelló.

Güell had acquired two large rural estates totalling fifteen hectares in the area popularly known as the Muntanya Pelada in the Gràcia District: Can Muntaner de Dalt, which he purchased from the Marqués de Marianao, and Can Coll i Pujol. At 450 to 630 feet above sea level, the property afforded attractive views over Barcelona, which was being extended in accordance with the Cerdà Plan over the length and breadth of the gently sloping plain. A number of contemporary engravings capture this fascinating panorama. The sixty-two housing plots planned for the park were to share community services, such as a caretaker and utilities. A marketplace, public square, and street system were also part of the master plan, but schools, hospitals, and other services were not.

For the first three years of construction, the principal task consisted of levelling the land. Gaudí wanted to alter the landscape as little as possible, so he ordered only essential earthworks and excavations. These self-imposed parameters obliged him to trace out a gentle network of roads which, wherever possible, followed the contours of the site. The main avenues are ten metres wide, with secondary thoroughfares of five and three metres in width. The arcades and viaducts supporting these roadways were constructed of stone excavated when the land was levelled, and merge into the terrain. Their various

designs evoke natural forms, such as palm trees. It is interesting to note that there are 150 large stone spheres lining the Carretera del Carmel, corresponding to the number of beads on a rosary.

Apart from the model house, the first residence to be built was for Martí Trias. Based on a project by Juli Batllevell, it was begun in 1903 and completed in 1906. That same year architect Francesc Berenguer designed a house for Gaudí and his father. Although Francesc Gaudí died shortly thereafter, Antoni remained in the house until 1925, when he resolved never to move from the Sagrada Família. These were the only plots to be sold, and as a residential estate the project was quickly deemed a resounding failure. As a public space, however, the park is a true masterpiece which, though incomplete in terms of its original brief, is a powerful artistic expression.

The complex was conceived as a vast stage set on which each element has a specific role to play as part of the intricately planned whole. A great rubblework wall with an undulating top covered in ceramic fragments borders the edge of the park in the sector by the entrance, which is its lowest point. In 1965, the original wooden entrance gates were replaced with wrought iron sections from the fence at Casa Vicens. A pair of large medallions spell out "Park Güell" in ceramic fragments. The main gate in Carrer d'Olot is flanked by two buildings, one of which was to be the caretaker's lodge, and the other a service pavilion. These distinctly vertical structures have oval ground plans. The plain rubblework buildings are finished off with fabulous

The Casa Gaudí,
designed in 1906 by
Francesc Berenguer
for Gaudí and his
father, is now
a museum.

Medallions set into
the perimeter wall
carry the name of
the park in English.

warped and crenellated roofs, embellished with designs composed of *trencadís de ceràmica*, broken ceramic tile. Both have central towers which act as ventilation shafts, crowned with perforated cowls that bring to mind the hallucinatory mushroom *amanita muscaria*. A thirty-six-foot undulated spire soars above the service pavilion, finishing in a cross, which was destroyed in 1936 and inadequately restored. These pavilions certainly recall fairy tales in the style of the Brothers Grimm, as they resemble storybook houses made of mounds of ice cream. It is not difficult to understand why surrealist Salvador Dalí, on first seeing such unorthodox and provocative buildings, imagined he had found a truly edible architecture. In the summer of 1995, during restoration work on what had been conceived as the caretaker's lodge, Gaudí's original interiors were discovered. They had been masked for decades by partitions and a false ceiling.

Immediately beyond the entrance gates a sinuous split staircase climbs up through the terraces of the park. On either side of the balustrades, which are covered in white ceramic fragments, rise curved crenellated walls decorated in a chequerboard pattern of tiles. A triangular garden and fountain divides the stairs at the base.

Halfway up, a great medallion fashioned of white and polychrome *trencadís* depicts a serpent emerging from the Catalan coat of arms. At the top of the stairs a giant lizard guards the grotto. It is said that once Gaudí had completed the sculpture's iron skeleton on which the ceramic decoration would be applied, he jumped up and down on it in order to break its domed shape and give the dragon the capriciously warped torso that has such expressive power. Perhaps the grotto, where one can pause on the ascent to the open air terrace, was Gaudí's evocation of the prehistoric cave filled with fossilised remains of large animals that was discovered on the site. He was known to be an enthusiast of such discoveries, and was particularly interested in caves, which he visited on his numerous hiking expeditions throughout Catalonia.

The hypostyle hall, originally designed to be a marketplace, is popularly known as the Hall of the Hundred Columns, although there are, in fact, only eighty-six. While the space has a dramatic impact, it seems too narrow and impractical to have ever functioned as a market. The sturdy, hollow Doric columns support the plaza above, which extends out over the colonnade like a huge visor. They also function as ducts, channeling

The caretaker's
lodge.

rainwater from the plaza to a cistern, the overflow of which runs through the dragon's mouth. The outermost columns lean in order to support the weight of the terrace. Their bases and the warped ceiling are covered in white *trencadís*. The rear colonnade was completed between 1903 and 1907; the front colonnade between 1907 and 1910.

Four columns have been left out, and in the spaces corresponding to where their capitals would touch the roof, Gaudí's collaborator, young architect Josep Maria Jujol, created spectacular polychromatic mosaics. Jujol gave free rein to an expressiveness quite different from that of his master, whose technique was more geometric and restrained. Jujol's work in the park can be easily identified because, unlike Gaudí, he was a consummate draughtsman and sketched out his designs. He was astonishingly avant-garde, even revolutionary, in his artistic vision and application of colours and materials. For the medallions, which he began in 1909, Jujol used not only the *trencadís* technique but also collage, which Picasso would not employ until 1912. He applied fragments of bottles, cups, glasses, and even a doll's head to these collages, giving several of them a highly sculptural form. Jujol's decoration of the marketplace is an indication of what he would achieve in the formidable piece of functional artwork he created above: the bench which undulates along the plaza's perimeter.

Gaudí allegedly developed the form for the ceramic bench by developing prefabricated modules based on the measurements of a seated workman. The bench was constructed between

Halfway up the stairs is a huge medallion with a serpent's head emerging from the Catalan flag.

1910 and 1913, and I would venture to propose that it was among the earliest abstract works of art in the twentieth century, particularly at this scale. As in the hall below, Gaudí provided the form and then gave Jujol absolute freedom to decorate it as he liked. Gaudí recognised that the artistic talent of his collaborator enriched his work and gave him a great deal of encouragement. While Gaudí established the basic rhythm of the composition in its undulating form, Jujol's contribution is like that of a great jazz soloist. Without limitations of any kind, he let his imagination take flight. Using a base of white or coloured ceramic fragments, he incorporated a great variety of elements: bas-reliefs, hand-painted discs, pieces of crockery from his father's house. He also included graffiti, not discovered until 1964, incising prayers to the Virgin and crosses in the

The lizard at the summit.

wet clay. Jujol applied colour to baked tiles, which were then baked again. Despite the fact that he inscribed his signature, claiming the work as his own, it was attributed to Gaudí until a few years ago. If this bench had been built in Paris, London, or Rome, I believe it would have been admired and acclaimed from the outset. Recognition in Spain came late, despite the fact that artists of the stature of Picasso, Dalí, Miró, Clavé, Tàpies, and Saura, to mention only Spaniards, have acknowledged its influence on their work. The contemporary painter Julian Schnabel has also said that the bench has been a source of inspiration.

The Park Güell is a true masterpiece, despite its immediate failure as a residential estate and the fact that it remains unfinished. Gaudí

Enclosing the plaza on the roof of the Hall
of the Hundred Columns is an undulating
wall that follows the roofline of the building.
On the plaza side, a bench with a richly
decorated back is incorporated in the wall.

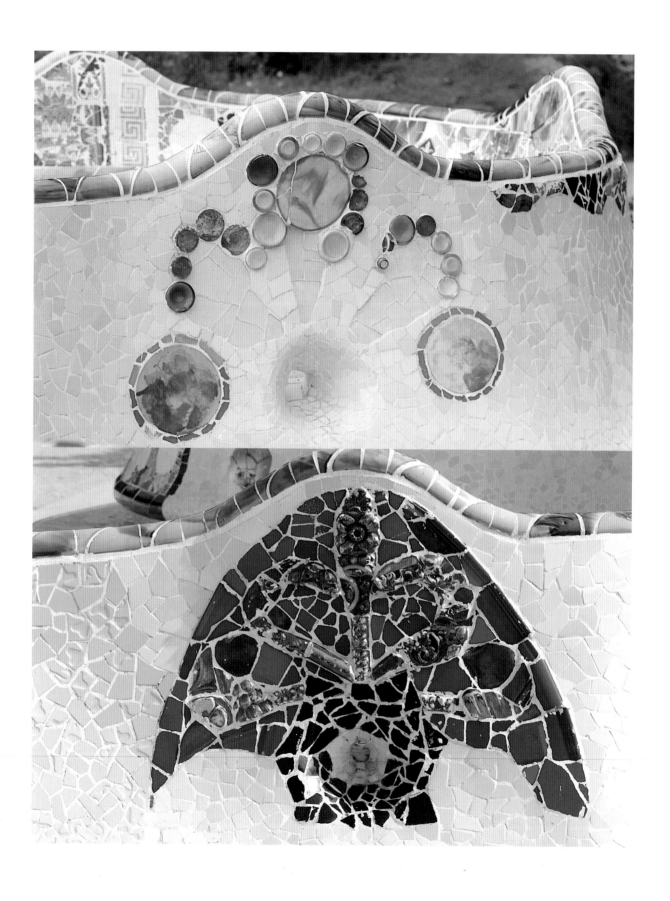

Jujol created the exuberant trencadis ornament for the bench.

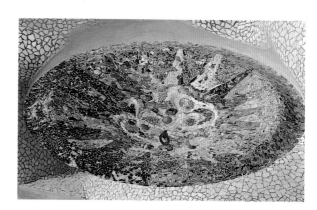

completed the work he was commissioned to undertake, and it is one of his most significant and most potent projects. From the time construction began, access to this private park was possible through payment of a modest fee, and it became a venue for public functions and festivities of all kinds. In 1906, for example, the "Garden Party" for the first Congress of the Catalan Language was held there. When

Eusebi Güell died, his heirs decided they did not want the responsibility of such a gigantic urban project and offered it for sale to the City Hall in 1922. Although there were voices raised in protest at the expenditure, the site was purchased and converted into a municipal park in 1923. The Park Güell was declared an artistic monument by the Barcelona civic authorities in 1962; in 1969, the Spanish Government declared it a

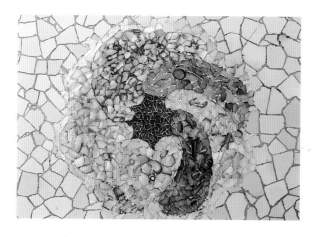

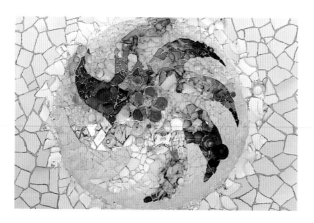

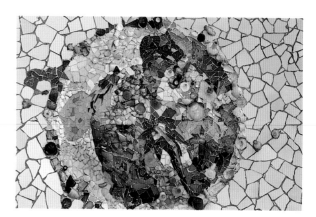

Parabolic arches beneath the viaduct create an ambiguous space.

An ornamental detail
characterised by a
curiously naïf accent.

national monument; and in 1984 it was included by UNESCO in the World Art Heritage list. The Amics de Gaudí association was able to acquire the architect's house in 1961. They established their headquarters there and in 1963 opened a museum. It primarily displays furniture, including pieces from Casa Calvet and Casa Batlló. The museum also possesses works by painter Aleix Clapés and sculptor Carles Mani, both of whom were among Gaudí's collaborators.

Bellesguard, la Casa Figueras

RONDA DE DALT
CARRER DE VALETA D'ARQUER
CARRER D'IRADIER
CARRER DE LA IMMACULADA
CARRER DELS PLANELLA
CARRER DE LES ESCOLES PIES
CARRER DE BELLESGUARD
CARRER DELS QUATRE CAMINS
CARRER DE JESÚS MARIA
CARRER DE SANT JOAN DE LA SALLE
PASSEIG DE LA BONANOVA
PLAÇA DE LA BONANOVA

Bellesguard, Casa Figueras
1900–1902

Carrer de Bellesguard, 16–20
Sarrià / Sant Gervasi District

Detail of ornamental tiles in the stair hall.

Bellesguard, Casa Figueras

In 1408, Martí I, the last Catalan monarch, chose this site for his summer residence. So esteemed by his subjects that he was called Martí "*l'humà*," Martí the Humane, the king suffered from chronic ill health. He had difficulty breathing, but his condition improved when he was in a dry climate; thus, when he was taken to this spot outside the city which commanded such a fine view of his beloved Barcelona, he immediately ordered a summer residence to be built. Martí I spent a great deal of time in this palace, which he christened Bellesguard for the beauty of its vista, and he received crowned heads of state and other dignitaries, including Pope Benedict XIII, there. The end of the Catalan royal line and subsequent political events led to the abandonment of this noble residence and its subsequent deterioration and collapse.

When Maria Sagués, the widow of Jaume Figueras, entrusted Gaudí with the Bellesguard project, all that was left of the original royal residence were the remains of two towers and a crenellated wall. This suited the architect, as these fragments gave wings to his imagination without restricting his creativity. He created a freely interpreted yet respectful evocation of the historical palace.

Gaudí began the project in 1900 by reconstructing the original wall and building a viaduct that allowed him to divert the road that crossed the estate. The plan was conceived as a square with fifteen-metre sides, and the house is finished with a narrow steeple crowned with the architect's sculptural interpretation of the Catalan flag. Exterior walls are constructed of rubblework and pieces of local slate. The use of these materials integrates the building with the landscape. In the narrow, tapered windows and crenellated roof line, Gaudí paid homage to the Catalan Gothic of the original castle. As in his tribute to *mudéjar* or Moorish decorative techniques at Casa Vicens, here at Bellesguard he created a wholly original work that evokes the spirit of an earlier style.

View from the garden and a detail of the principal facade.

The entrance. The mosaics flanking the gate were designed by Domènc Sugrañes.

It is unfortunate that the interior cannot be seen. In composition and plan it anticipates by several decades what Le Corbusier called the *promenade architectonique*. At Bellesguard, Gaudí realised the aesthetic potential of structural elements, showing them off rather than concealing them. Light filtering through colored glass panes onto white walls, and unexpectedly beautiful rough brick arches in the attic are among the details which contribute to the interior aesthetic.

Architect Domènec Sugrañes i Gras assisted Gaudí on this project, and carried out a number of unfortunate decorative additions—albeit with Gaudí's consent. Among the most inappropriate are the mosaics on the bench backrests on either side of the entrance gate; these designs are thoroughly out of place. Bellesguard is in a fine state of repair thanks to the commitment of its present owners, the family of Lluís Aguilera.

A courtyard
and a curved seat
in the garden.

In keeping with the
history of the palace,
Gaudi evoked the
Gothic style in the
details of the facade.

The stair hall is filled with light and color.

*Clockwise from upper left:
The attic vaulting; a
sculptural interpretation of
the Catalan flag atop the
principal spire; a passage
behind the crenellations;
view from the spire.*

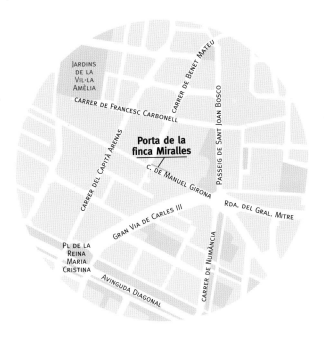

The Gate to the Finca Miralles

1901–1902

Passeig de Manuel Girona, 55–57
Sarrià / Sant Gervasi District

At the turn of the century, Hermenegild Miralles, a printer and publisher, asked Gaudí to design an enclosure for a large estate he owned in Sarrià. Miralles and Gaudí had a long-standing friendship, and on one occasion Miralles had tested the resistance of certain stone columns by subjecting them to the weight of one of his presses at the architect's request. Gaudí designed a sinuous rubblework wall topped with a railing that followed the same rhythm. Unfortunately, much of the

The gate with contemporary apartment blocks beyond.

wall was knocked down in 1956, and the railing was removed a few years later. The entrance gate, which still stands in Passeig de Manuel Girona, has undulating surfaces and is crowned with a wrought-iron cross. The enclosure was endowed with a dynamism unusual for such a simple project.

CARRER DE PROVENÇA

CARRER DE MALLORCA

PASSEIG DE GRÀCIA

CARRER DE VALÈNCIA

RAMBLA DE CATALUNYA

CARRER DE PAU CLARIS

CARRER DE ROGER DE LLÚRIA

Casa Batlló

CARRER D'ARAGÓ

CARRER DE BALMES

CARRER DEL CONSELL DE CENT

CARRER DE LA DIPUTACIÓ

GRAN VIA DE LES CORTS CATALANES

Casa Batlló
1904–1907

Passeig de Gràcia, 43
L'Eixample District

Detail of the decoration of principal facade created with ceramic discs and fragments of coloured glass.

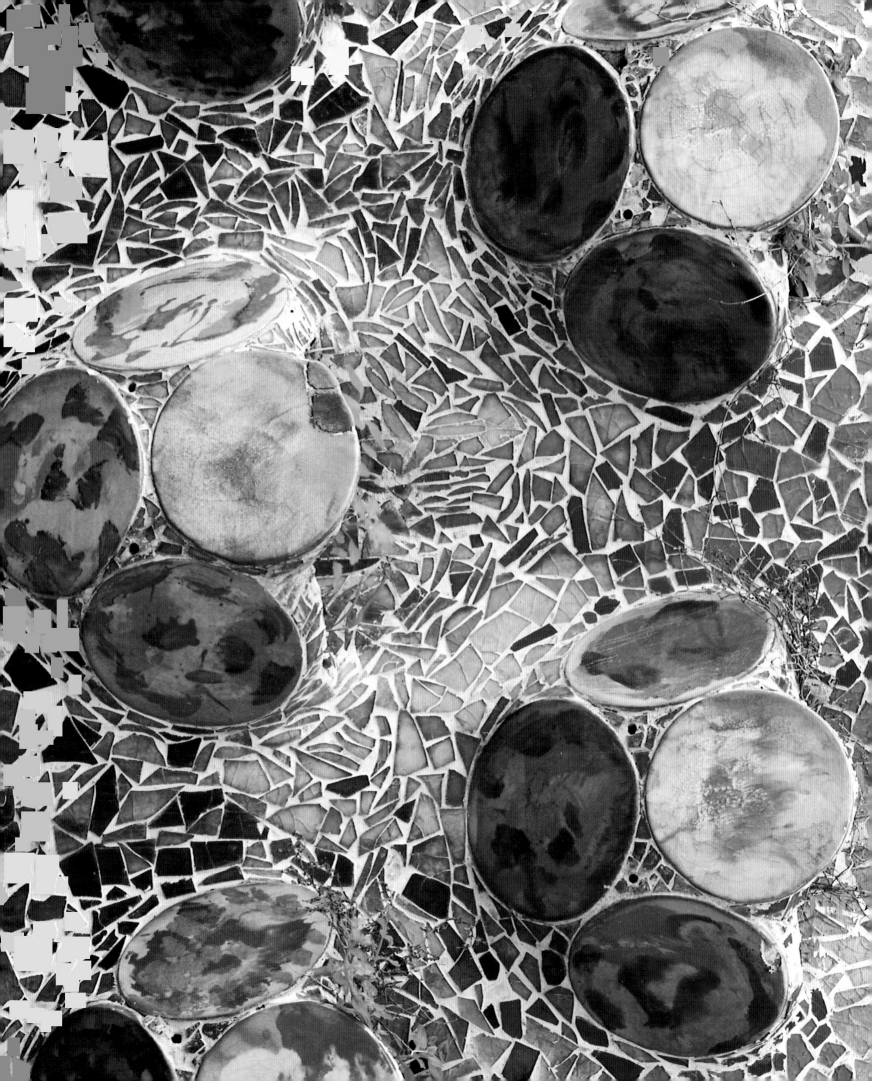

Casa Batlló

In 1904, Gaudí was commissioned by Josep Batlló Casanovas to make dramatic alterations to a building he owned on the fashionable Passeig de Gràcia. Originally Batlló had requested permission from the City Hall to demolish the

building, Casa Luis Sala Sánchez, which dated from 1875 and was of little architectural interest. For unknown reasons, he ended up retaining much of the original structure. Ultimately, Gaudí designed a new facade for the building, added a fifth floor, and greatly altered the interior.

Casa Batlló was situated between Casa Amatller, designed by Puig i Cadafalch, and Casa Lleó i Morera, designed by Domènech i Montaner. The facades of these three buildings, which could be viewed together from across the wide avenue, were so diverse that their block was christened the Mançana de la Discòrdia, the Apple (or Block) of Discord, a play on words of the kind so popular with the people of Barcelona. The citizens closely followed the progress of the facade's construction, as they had come to expect original, imaginative work from the architect. Gaudí did not disappoint them at Casa Batlló. As soon as it was complete it became known popularly as the Casa dels Ossos, or House of Bones. Bearing in mind that the ironwork was originally painted an ivory colour, and the stone, extracted from the quarries of Montjuïc, was of a natural vanilla tone, this is an appropriate name. Some historians have understood the design to be an evocation of Carnival, with the balustrades as masks, the multicoloured tiles of the facade as confetti, and the crest as a harlequin's cap. I do not believe that one as devout as Gaudí would have chosen such a pagan festival as his inspiration. Others see the facade as a representation of the shimmering sea which bathes the shallow coves of the Costa Brava.

The symbolism I detect in this spectacular composition derives from the legend of Sant Jordi (St. George), patron saint of Catalonia. The tower can be seen to represent his lance, crowned by a three-dimensional cross embodying the

View from Passeig de Gràcia.

A huge stained-glass window floods the interior with coloured light.

The shape and ivory color of the blaustrades suggested the nickname "House of Bones."

triumph of good over evil, a religious principle beloved by Gaudí. The body of the tower features the gilded initials of Jesus (JHS), Joseph (JHP), and Mary (M). The lance has mortally wounded the dragon, represented here by the scale-like roof tiles and shimmering facade. The wound itself is the hollow inset to the left of the tower; the dragon's scales and spine (the ridge line of the roof) are even coloured blood-red. The balcony balustrades recall the eye sockets of skulls, and elements of the lower part of the facade bring to mind the bones of the dragon's victims.

From the entrance hall a staircase leads directly up to the first floor, where Batlló and his family resided. These quarters were meticulously conceived by Gaudí to meet the needs of his client, and he considered no detail unimportant. One

of Batlló's grandchildren by marriage once told me that Gaudí had inquired how many men and how many women were in the family. Batlló's

wife thought this strange and demanded an explanation. Gaudí responded that he intended to design different chairs for each sex, based on their attire, not their anatomy. She would have none of it, and thus Gaudí designed the "unisex" chairs that can be admired today.

Outstanding craftsmen contributed to the project, including the Badía brothers, who were responsible for the wrought iron; the firm of Casas y Bardés for the joinery; Hijo de P. Pujol Baucís for the tiling; Sebastià Ribó for the ceramics; and Josep Pelegrí for the stained glass. The discs on the facade and the cladding for the cross were the work of Manacor. I believe it is possible to detect the intervention of Gaudí's collaborator, Josep Maria Jujol, although it is not documented. I see his hand above all in the abstract ornamentation of the main facade, which shows his characteristic spontaneity and his provocative, avant-garde approach to a surface. Historians Joan Bassegoda and Antonio González deny that Jujol was involved in this project; however, Ignasi de Solà-Morales and Flores, the curators of an exhibition of his work organised by the Col·legi d'Arquitectes, contend that he did contribute to the polychrome decoration of the facade. My opinion is based on the stylistic similarities I find in this facade and other work known to be his.

As at Bellesguard, this house invites us to enjoy a *promenade architectonique* long before those of Le Corbusier, beginning in the vestibule, continuing up the staircase to the landing, proceeding through the waiting room, and ending in the private quarters. Certain elements of the building, despite their essential simplicity, are particularly noteworthy, such as the subtle gradation of color from deep blue to white in the interior patio, which varies depending on the intensity of the

The stair hall is richly decorated with tile.

The interior court is faced with blue tiles, whose colour varies depending on the intensity of the light from above.

Interior of the Batlló apartment.

natural light. While the rear facade is not spectacular, it merits contemplation due to the effect Gaudí achieved in the pattern of solids and voids, and the multicoloured ornamentation. The recently restored attic is a spectacular space in which the potency of the exposed structure, the graceful parabolic arches, is revealed. Gaudí's sculptural treatment of chimney groups such as these has evolved from Palau Güell and culminates at Casa Milà. Here the chimneys are decorated with patterns of brightly coloured tiles.

The ground-floor level of Casa Batlló has recently been converted into a space which can be hired for meetings, conventions, and all manner of social functions. If we want certain old buildings to stay alive, we must refurbish and adapt them to new uses. In this case, the people of Barcelona and others who appreciate Gaudí's work now have the opportunity to visit a private property that had been closed to them.

While the cost of altering Casa Batlló was much higher than anticipated, due to Gaudí's penchant for designing while building, and while Batlló knew from personal experience that dealing with Gaudí required infinite patience, as he was strongminded and often prickly, he still recommended the architect to his friend and business partner Milà, who had also decided to build a house on Passeig de Gràcia. And so it was that in 1906, as he finishing Casa Batlló, Gaudí began work on Casa Milà, which the people of Barcelona quickly christened La Pedrera, The Quarry.

Doors in Batllò apartment.

The hearth provides an unexpected private space.

Doorway to the rear courtyard (opposite).

The rear facade and details of the top-floor balcony and decorated chimneys (opposite and following pages).

CARRER DE BONAVISTA

AVINGUDA DIAGONAL

CARRER DE CÓRSEGA

CARRER DE BALMES

CARRER DE ROSSELLÓ

PASSEIG DE GRÀCIA

Casa Milà, La Pedrera

CARRER DEL BRUC

RAMBLA DE CATALUNYA

CARRER DE PROVENÇA

CARRER DE ROGER DE LLÚRIA

CARRER DE MALLORCA

CARRER DE PAU CLARIS

CARRER DE VALÈNCIA

CARRER D'ARAGÓ

Casa Milà, La Pedrera

1906–1910

Passeig de Gràcia, 92
L'Eixample District

*Detail of a wall excuted in Jujol's
pure sculptural style.*

148

Casa Milà, La Pedrera

On the large asymmetrical plot at the corner of Passeig de Gràcia, 92, and Carrer de Provença, 261–265, stood the Casa Josep Antonio Ferrer-Vidal, a residence surrounded by a garden. Pedro Milà Camps purchased the property, and in 1906

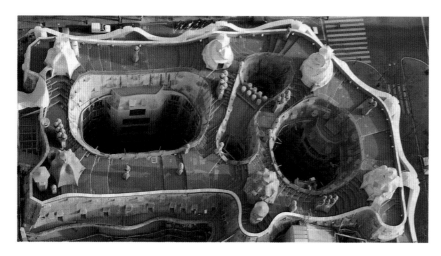

The principal facade and an aerial view of the roof

commissioned Gaudí to demolish the existing structure and design an apartment building for the site. Milà was married to Roser Segimon, widow of the rich *indiano* Guardiola, a Catalan who had made his fortune in the Americas and brought it back to Spain. Milà was the object of barbed speculation in Barcelona society at the time, as people wondered whether he had married the Guardiola widow, or the widow's *guardiola*, her moneybox.

There have been many theories as to Gaudí's inspiration for this project. Some see an evocation of the ocean's waves, and others see it as a mountain crowned by a cloud. While many agree that the mountains provided him with his imagery, they differ as to the specific peaks. Joan Bergós believes he had in mind Fra Gerau, in the Prades mountains, which were familiar from his childhood. Joan Matamala thought it might have been Sant Miquel del Fai, which Gaudí had visited on one of his many hiking excursions. The sculptor Vicente Vilarrubias was inclined to believe it was the mountain and beach of Pareis, while others favour Calescobes in Menorca. In his exhaustive study, Tokutoshi Torii reproduces a number of exotic images of peaks he considers to be possibilities, and Juan Goytisolo, more of a novelist than an historian, imagines it to be distant Capadocia.

My belief is that he was inspired by the highly unusual and impressive crest of Sant Sadurní, which rises above Gallifa in the Vallès Occidental region. A series of circumstances indicates that Gaudí would have had first-hand knowledge of this peak. According to historian Joan Bassegoda i Nonell in his biography of Gaudí, a cholera epidemic broke out in Barcelona

The wrought-iron balconies on the facade overlooking the interior courtyard were the creation of Jujol.

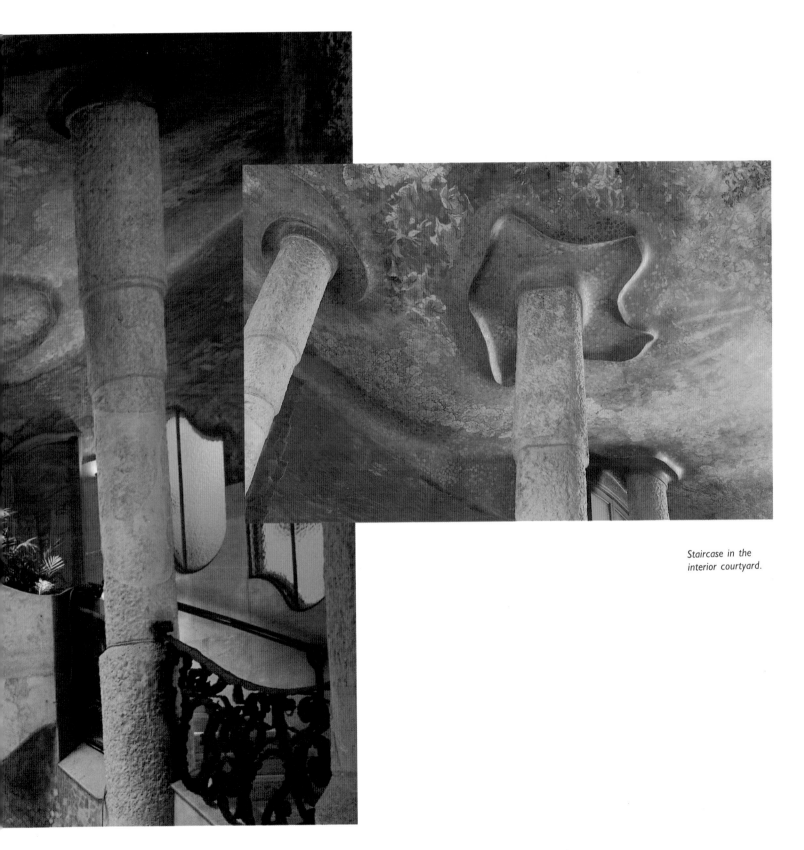

Staircase in the interior courtyard.

View through the
entrance gate
to the street.

A painted ceiling
off the interior
courtyard.

in 1885, causing 1,318 deaths in less than a year. The architect decided to seek refuge in Sant Feliu de Codines, where he spent a considerable amount of time. He stayed with Frances Ullar, for whom he designed a dining room table. He also gave advice on the construction of the Roca Umbert textile factory, and in 1900 was asked by textile industrialist Emili Carles Tolrà to design the standard of the Orfeó Feliuà, which is preserved in the Sant Feliu Town Hall.

It is highly probable that Gaudí would have taken advantage of this temporary exile to devote himself to hiking, which was his favourite hobby. One popular route leads to the hermitage of Sant Sadurní, perched atop a crest just behind the village of Gallifa, which is only eight kilometres from Sant Feliu de Codines and is now justly famous as the site of Llorens Artigas' ceramic atelier. The hermitage stands at 2,820 feet above sea level, and from that point it is possible to enjoy a view so impressive that it has remained fresh in my memory since childhood. While the Sant Sadurní massif is visible from Sant Feliu, its menacing rounded forms crowned by a wide, undulating frieze become increasingly awesome as one approaches. It is interesting to observe that not only does the massif have a chamfered corner similar to the one at Casa Milà, it extends asymmetrically as the building does along Carrer de Provença.

Whatever the inspiration, Casa Milà must be understood as Gaudí's attempt to create not only a functional apartment building, or a fine unorthodox design, but a complete sculpture. In this context, I would like to stress the fact that Jujol, his collaborator, did more than simply interpret this intention; his contribution was essential to its successful resolution. Striking evidence

of this is the sculptural dimension with which Jujol endowed the balcony railings. Each is wholly original, improvised in the forge, and there is a vast difference between the natural, expressive quality of these railings and the controlled, modular repetition of the entrance doors on the ground floor, which were designed by Gaudí. Jujol's work enriches the project far more than certain decorative elements designed by Gaudí himself. Jujol's railings, by virtue not only of their form but also their colour, create a counterpoint to the smooth facade, contrasting stone and iron, pale ochre and black, solid mass and gestural openwork, density and aerial evanescence. Jujol's mastery of ironwork in architectural detailing inspired two Catalan sculptors, Pau Gargallo and Juli González, to employ this material in sculpture for the first time, thus giving this material its rightful place in the history of art. González ultimately taught Picasso the technique.

Casa Milà is actually two buildings, each arranged around a curvilinear central patio, and each with a separate entrance. The facade is composed of large blocks of stone, from Garraf on the lower floors, and Vilafranca on the floors above. Each of the blocks was dressed on site and then fitted into the ensemble. In order to achieve the coherent sculptural unity he sought, Gaudí made major changes throughout the process, which was typical of his working methods. If one of the characteristics of the *modernista* period was indeed a lack of structural innovation, Casa Mila is not only avant-garde but truly revolutionary in this respect. Thanks to a framework of pillars and steel girders, Gaudí was able to eliminate bearing walls, and thus could alter the distribution of space on each floor as much as he liked.

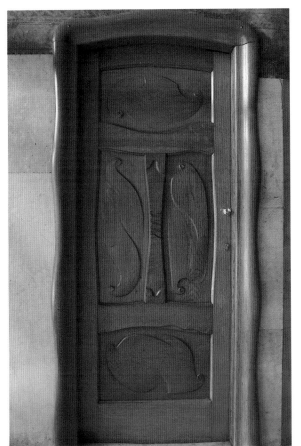

Decorative details in wood, glass, and wrought iron, all designed by Gaudí.

The same asymmetry that governs the facade also characterises the interior.

The facade has three well-differentiated parts: the six floors marked by the sinuous arrangement of stone blocks; the two-level attic which is set back and is further distinguished from the body of the building by changes in surface rhythm, material, and colour; and the flat roof. The attic facade is made of smooth, white stones set at an angle, punctured by irregularly spaced window openings. The set-back creates a "sentry walk" on the roof of the main structure. Along the undulating cornice Gaudí had inscribed: *Ave gratia M plena Dominus tecum*, his homage to the Virgin. Just below the initial "M," which could refer to Mary, is a rosebud. According to Bassegoda, Gaudí was dissatisfied with the sculptor's execution of this form and made him redo it several times.

Above the initial, Gaudí had intended to place a sculptural group to crown the building. Carles Mani, a protégé and collaborator of the architect, modelled a figure of the Virgin and Child flanked by the Archangel Michael, who, with his sword, triumphs over Evil, and the Archangel Gabriel, who offers Mary the lily of purity. The work, cast in gilded bronze, was never executed, which has generated a host of speculations. Some said the sculpture was to be as big as the building itself; in fact Mani's piece was only four metres high. Others said the Milà family was so fearful of the events of *Setmana Tràgica*, Tragic Week, that they dared not display an image that might be seen as a provocation. Bassegoda has shown that this interpretation cannot be correct as the chronology of events does not follow. The truth is far more prosaic: the Milàs simply hated the sculpture and refused to put it up. This disagreement was one of the many bitter differences between client and architect; ultimately Gaudí sued them for his fees. He won the case and gave the money to charity so that everyone would know he had fought solely for principles. For my part, I think it is best that the sculpture was never executed. From the drawing Matamala made of it years later, it is obvious that it would have clashed terribly with the pure avant-garde style of the building. Mani's piece was like something out of a sentimental Nativity scene, a quality that characterizes many of the Sagrada Família sculptures, although in that context they create no discord.

Gaudí's sculptural treatment of rooftop elements, first explored at Palau Güell, and later Casa Batlló, culminates at Casa Milà. Here the architect created striking, imposing forms which can be appreciated not only at the rooftop level, but also from the street. Thus, they are an integral part of the entire composition and contribute to the building's dramatic impact. The roof consists of several levels and supports three functions: stair entrances, of which there are six; ventilation shafts; and chimneys. The stair entrances take the form of huts crowned by large helmets. As was so often the case, practical requirements did not dictate conventional forms for Gaudí; on the contrary, he brought his highly personal vision to the task, seeking forms that would please him. Each staircase is individually detailed. The sinuous ridges on the surface of one hut look as though they were created by the lashing of a whip, and it is crowned by the three-dimensional cross often found in the architect's work. The curved rooftops of the stair entrances are clad in fragments of marble tiling. The ventilators' forms herald the abstract sculpture of

The facade
overlooking the
interior courtyard.

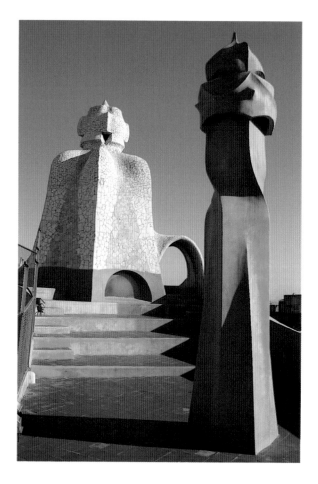

subsequent decades, and their pattern of openings emphasises void over solid. The chimneys are reminiscent of those at Casa Batlló, where a striking form becomes more impressive when grouped with others of its kind. Here the chimneys can be seen as the helmeted heads of warriors; indeed, they bring to my mind the knights entering battle in Eisenstein's magnificent film *Alexander Nevsky*. The cladding of one chimney consists of fragments of champagne bottles. The sculptural

elements of this rooftop differ from those at Palau Güell in that they are fairly monochromatic; the ceramic fragments applied to the surface have been chosen from a limited colour range. A visit to this roof, from which it is possible to see both Casa Batlló and the Sagrada Família, is an unforgettable experience.

The individual apartments in the building, some of which were detailed by Gaudí and Jujol, are

Chimneys take on forms of abstract sculpture.

highly varied. Jujol traced words reflecting his passionate religious beliefs in the surfaces of some columns. Although no evidence remains, we know that in some rooms Jujol went further in his artistic expression, impulsively hurling pots of paint at certain walls, a technique based on *tachisme*, which was in keeping with his methods. He also contributed to the designs of arches and window details, and designed certain pieces of furniture. Among other details, Gaudí designed the

mezzanine railings, a combination of bench, cupboard, and handrail; the mosaic later used to pave Passeig de Gràcia; and the apartment doors. Some of these elements are preserved in the Museum-House in Park Güell.

When Gaudí died in 1926, all traces of his work were erased from the Milàs' private apartments on the first floor. Milà's wife, Roser Segimon, had taken an intense dislike to the

*Jujol endowed a
simple interplay of
curves and reliefs
with majesty.*

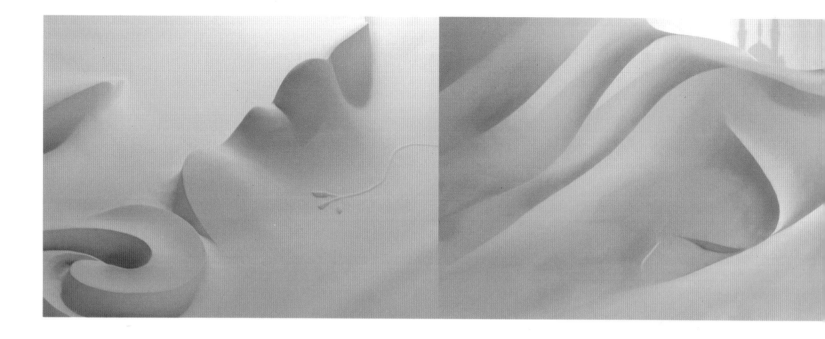

architect and replaced his decoration with a decor in the style of Louis XVI. Some years ago, when the Caixa de Catalunya Savings Bank acquired the building, Jujol's detailing of the columns and ceilings was rediscovered and can now be admired when the space is open for exhibitions.

In 1956, architect Barba Corsini transformed the attics into modern penthouses, and his alterations showed great respect for the original space. In 1993 new owners decided to restore the attic to its original form; this powerful space now accommodates a permanent exhibition of Gaudí's work. The basement has also been modified. Gaudí had originally conceived it as a stable and coach house, but by the time the first tenants moved in it was clear that new forms of transport required new solutions. The industrialist Feliu, who owned a Rolls Royce, informed the architect that a column prevented him from taking his car into the basement. Gaudí himself

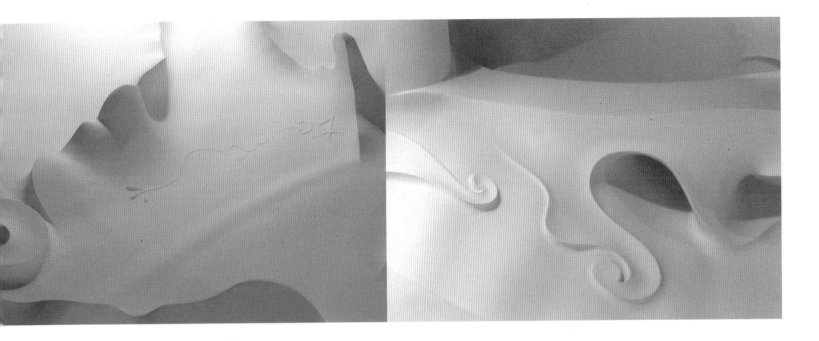

oversaw the alterations, although he confessed that the operation was more difficult than the construction of the entire Carrer de Provença facade. In the early sixties, the space was used for a fashion flea market. At the beginning of 1995, the Caixa de Catalunya inaugurated an auditorium there. While it does dignify the space, I am not convinced that the decorative style is appropriate, as it does not harmonise with the rest of the building. The same entity also undertook the restoration of the murals in the vestibules. Their authorship had always been in question. Research undertaken in 1995 by Josep M. Carandell revealed that the painter had copied themes from the series of Brussels tapestries based on Ovid's *Metamorphosis*, that are now owned by the Art Heritage of Spain. The Casa Milà paintings are thoroughly unremarkable. Subsequent research by Joan Bassegoda revealed that the owners had given carte blanche to painter Aleix Clapés, whom they much admired. Without consulting Gaudí, Clapés chose the

View from the
roof to the
Sagrada Família.

themes and commissioned Iu Pasqual, Xavier Nogués, and Teresa Lostau to execute them. Clapés was also involved in the decoration of the Milàs' private apartments.

That Casa Milà was an exceptional work became clear even before it was completed. A municipal bureaucrat reported that the building did not comply with regulations governing dimensions, but the matter was resolved by a forward-looking City Council, which recognised La Pedrera's outstanding quality. A further problem arose when another official found that one of the columns jutted out into Passeig de Gràcia. When Gaudí retorted that he refused to cut off that "leg," and that, furthermore, if he were forced to do so by municipal order he would erect a placard stating who was responsible for such a brutal mutilation, the matter was dropped. There were those, however, who did not recognise the extraordinary quality of Casa Milà. Among them were members of the jury who annually granted architecture awards: they did not even consider this work by Gaudí the year it was completed. In 1961, Casa Milà, La Pedrera, was included in the Barcelona City Hall's catalogue of monuments; in 1969, it was declared a national monument; and in 1984, it was included by UNESCO in the World Art Heritage list.

The Temple of the Sagrada Família

1882–1926

Carrer Marina, 253
Carrer Provença, 450
Carrer Mallorca, 403
L'Eixample District

*Detail of the modernista curve
of the spiral staircase.*

The Temple
of the
Sagrada Família

The Expiatory Temple of the Holy Family, the Sagrada Família church, is Gaudí's most ambitious and best-known project, a work to which he devoted himself from the early years of his career until his death. It is the most controversial creation of a man who invited controversy. Even now, many years after his death, the debate continues, centering on how this unfinished work has been carried on.

In 1866, a pious bookseller named Josep María Bocabella Verdaguer founded the Asociación Espiritual de los Devotos de San José, the purpose of which was to strengthen the position of the Catholic Church in Barcelona, which he felt had been eroded. He received the blessing of the Vatican, and vigorously pursued his mission. In 1874, Bocabella and his priest, the Mercedarian Josep María Rodríguez, conceived the idea that a church should be built at the initiative of the Asociación, which would be dedicated to the Holy Family as the model of the virtues of domestic life, St. Joseph as the patron of the working class, and the expiation of the sins of a material age. They raised money from the members to purchase the land and begin the project. The property they could afford was, at the time, on the outskirts of Barcelona; by the time Gaudí became involved in the project, the site was part of the rapidly growing, highly fashionable Eixample district. Bocabella approached architect Francisco de Paula del Villar i Lozano, who drew up the plans free of charge. The design he rendered was for a neo-Gothic structure, which was to be the nucleus of a complex that would include gardens, schools, recreation rooms, and other services. In 1882, construction began on the crypt. Soon, however, difficulties arose between del Villar and architect Joan Martorell, the works director, and del Villar resigned. Martorell recommended that the young Gaudí, who had apprenticed with him, take over the project. Gaudí radically altered the project in style and in scope.

The Sagrada Família occupies an entire block in the Eixample, and is surrounded by open space allowing it to be contemplated from a distance. Opposite the Passion Facade is the Plaça de la Sagrada Família, and facing opposite the Nativity Facade is the Plaça de Gaudí. This is remarkable in a city as densely built as Barcelona. The church, which is constructed of sandstone from Montjuïc, takes the form of a Latin cross in plan, with a wide nave of five aisles, a transept of three aisles, and an apse. There are seven chapels off the ambulatory, dedicated to baptism, penitence, the theological virtues, the sorrows, and St. Joseph's verses in honour of the Virgin. A cloister which was to encircle the entire church was one of Gaudí's additions to the original design.

Gaudí imagined a structure of strong verticality, an apotheosis of eighteen spires representing the twelve Apostles, the four Evangelists, the Virgin, and Christ, who would have been symbolised by a tower soaring over five hundred feet. He intended to install a system of bells in the towers which would have been activated by the force of the wind. Three facades were to illustrate with sculptural images the Nativity, the Passion, and the Resurrection of Christ. The iconography of the exterior was rich and complex in its conception; a profusion of elements, from numbers and symbols to representational sculpture, were to convey a multitude of messages. Light is as fundamental to this structure as the stone used to build it. Gaudí conceived the interior of the church as a vast forest of columns flooded with light.

As was characteristic of his working methods, Gaudí set to work exclusively on the Nativity Facade without having drawn up an overall plan for the temple. His intention was to compose a narrative of the Birth of Christ, enriching it with Christian iconography as well as fantastic and geometric elements. The facade is arranged around three main portals, which represent Hope, Charity, and Faith. The Hope Portal depicts the anagram of St. Joseph; the wedding of the Virgin and St. Joseph; the Flight into Egypt; the Slaughter of the Innocents; and Egyptian flora, including lilies, palms, jasmine, and the Joshua tree. At the top of the door are the Apostle Barnaby, whose pinnacle is crowned by the Holy Spirit and the Milky Way, and the Apostle Simon, with motifs of the mountain of Montserrat. The central Charity Portal depicts the anagram of Jesus; the angels of the Annunciation; the Nativity scene; the star of Bethlehem; the coronation of the Virgin; the Eucharist; chaos; the mineral world; and the plant world. These images are surmounted by pinnacles containing the apostles Simon and Thaddeus. Above all is a gigantic cypress tree in green ceramic. On the Faith Portal we find the anagram of Mary; Jesus in the Temple; Jesus the carpenter; and the vegetation of Palestine. The Immaculate Conception, the Holy Trinity, and the lantern of Faith finish off this doorway. Some critics of the densely packed multiplicity of images in this facade have played off the word for Nativity, *Belén*, which also means "bedlam."

It seems inconceivable that Gaudí would have used such unremarkable pseudo-classical sculpture in a work that had such transcendent meaning for him. It is my belief that his appreciation of representational sculpture was not as finely tuned as that of the other arts. Otherwise he would not have been content with the services of Carles Mani, Joan Busquets, and Joan Matamala, and

Interior view of the apse and eastern transept of the Church (unfinished).

Crowning the Nativity facade is this massive cypress tree executed in green ceramic.

would have sought other artists. Gaudí was known to have obtained moulds for his sculptures from actual objects, as well as animals and people, and sometimes even corpses. There is abundant documentation of this practice, and of his use of a system in which he surrounded the model with a circle of mirrors so that the sculptor could see all possible angles of a pose. Good sculpture is rarely, if ever, attained by such methods. It seems that Gaudí sought realism in these works, and that is why he meticulously chose the individual models and used this pedestrian approach.

One of the many sculptures on the Nativity Facade depicts an anarchist, complete with bomb.

While this may at first seem out of context, it does have an explanation. The building is, after all, an expiatory temple. Its founders and followers believed that Barcelona had to atone for her anti-clerical and violently anti-religious sins, many of which were quite recent. Gaudí himself had witnessed the events of the *Setmana Tràgica*. From the fifties onward, some among the faithful took exception to the original expiatory charge, believing that it ran counter to the Catholic Church's message of reconciliation.

Such considerations led, in the sixties, to reflections on whether the construction of Sagrada Família should cease. Beyond issues

The imposing spiral staircase within the spire.

of ideological nuance, there has been concern as to whether work should continue from an aesthetic standpoint. When he was killed by a tram in 1926, Gaudí left no detailed plans for the execution of the church as he conceived it, and when the Civil War broke out, what little documentation there was, including models and sketches, was destroyed. At the end of the conflict, some restoration work was carried out on sculptural elements that had been damaged. Since 1949, thanks to funds raised by donations, the work has gone on. At one point Le Corbusier proposed that the temple be completed using a neutral material, such as glass, so that the building could at last be functional. In the mid-sixties a manifesto was published in the review *Destino*, signed by numerous prominent individuals from around the world, requesting that the work be stopped. It proceeded, nonetheless. The controversy was rekindled in 1986, when Josep Maria Subirachs was asked to create a major sculptural group to preside over the Passion Facade. Demonstrations were organised in protest of the pieces he executed, but they were not removed. Since Gaudí's death, several architects have considered themselves to be is heirs, and have dared to carry on. The work continues as funds accumulate, primarily from the sale of entrance tickets to tourists. While Gaudí himself expressed his intention that work on the church would be continued by future generations, he left them no guidelines. To say that the construction of cathedrals has always been a collective effort does not really address the issue here. Sagrada Família is the highly personal creation of an improvisational genius who, while he had collaborators, trained no disciples.

Biographical Summary

1852   Antoni Gaudí i Cornet, son of a Riudoms cooper, is born on June 25 in Reus.

1869   Moves to Barcelona to complete his secondary school education.

1873   Begins to study architecture and collaborates with the master builder Fontserè.

1876   Works as a draughtsman for the architect Francisco de Paula del Villar.

1878   Qualifies as an architect; makes his first contact with Eusebi Güell.

1891   Travels to León and Astorga for the projects for Casa de los Botines and the Episcopal Palace.

1903   Travels to Mallorca to restore the Cathedral.

1905   Moves to the Park Güell with his father and his niece.

1906   Death of his father.

1911   Contracts Maltese fever. Recovers in Puigcerdà.

1912   Death of his niece.

1926   June 7: Fatally injured by a tram. June 12: Buried in the crypt of the Sagrada Família.

Selected Bibliography

BASSEGODA NONELL, Juan. *Gaudí*. Salvat, Barcelona, 1985.
— *La Pedrera de Gaudí*. Caixa de Catalunya, Barcelona. 1987.
— *El gran Gaudí*. Ausa, Sabadell, 1989.

BERGÓS, Joan. *Antoni Gaudí: l'home i l'obra*. Ariel, Barcelona, 1954.

BOHIGAS, Oriol. *Arquitectura modernista*. Lumen, Barcelona, 1968.

CASANELLAS, Enric. *Nueva visión de Gaudí*. Polígrafa, Barcelona, 1964.

CIRICI PELLICER, Alexandre. *El arte modernista catalán*. Aymà, Barcelona, 1951.

CIRLOT, Juan Eduardo. *El arte de Gaudí*. Omega, Barcelona, 1950.

Several authors. *Josep Maria Jujol, arquitecte. 1879–1949*. Col·legi d'Arquitectes, Barcelona, 1989.
— *El Palau Güell*. Diputació de Barcelona, Barcelona, 1990.

FLORES, Carlos. *Gaudí, Jujol y el modernismo catalán*. Aguilar, Madrid, 1982.

MARTINELL, César: *Gaudinismo*. Amigos de Gaudí, Barcelona, 1954.
— *Gaudí: su vida, su teoría, su obra*. Colegio de Arquitectos, Barcelona, 1967.

PERMANYER, Lluís. *Història de l'Eixample*. Plaza y Janés, Barcelona, 1991.
— *Cites i testimonis sobre Barcelona*. La Campana, Barcelona, 1993.
— *Biografia del Passeig de Gràcia*. 1994.

PUJOLS, Francesc; Salvador DALÍ; Robert DESCHARNES; Clovis PREVOST. *La visió artística i religiosa de Gaudí*. Aymà, Barcelona, 1969.

RÀFOLS, Josep Francesc. *Modernismo y modernistas*. Destino, Barcelona, 1949.

SOLÀ-MORALES, Ignasi de. *Gaudí*. Polígrafa, Barcelona, 1983.

Chronological Index of works